170
G226s
1996

2/96

spirit speaks TO sisters

SPIRIT SPEAKS TO SISTERS

An Empowering Testimony of Faith and Love
for Women of African Ascent

reverent JUNE JULIET GATLIN

THE NOBLE PRESS, INC. ~ *Chicago*

Designed by Al Brandtner
Cover illustration by Melverue Abraham

Printed in the United States of America

Library of Congress Cataloguing–in–Publication Data

Gatlin, June J.
    Spirit speaks to sisters: an empowering testimony of faith
    and love for women of African ascent/June J. Gatlin
        p.   cm.
    ISBN 1–879360—39–X
1. Spiritual life 2. Afro–Americans—Religion
3. Self–esteem in women—United States
HQ800.4.U6D38   1996
646.7'7'098996073–dc20

The Noble Press, Inc.
213 W. Institute Place, Suite 407
Chicago, IL 60610

To my son, Anthony Del Patrick Thompkins and his daughter,
Aubrini Zuriah Thompkins. God told me they would be born.
The promise was kept. The word became flesh.
Praise RAHUYWHYHVHALAYAH.

To Big Ma, my beloved grandmother Adeline Jones Hale,
and her first born, Alice. My mother, when pregnant,
prayed that the gift be passed to me because she didn't want it.
I am her first born, eldest of nine and inheritor of the vision.

To our stalwart vision keepers and to those whom many have hoped would keep silent, to those who become pregnant with words, daring to give birth to liberators, scientists, soil tillers, orators and archeologists, to our astronauts and poets, philosophers, engineers and explorers, to all richly creative talents who are determined to found and erect new kingdoms, to our blessed minds, and to our ancestors, our prolific progenitors whom we must uncover, discover and honor; and to our First World ascendants, children of the ancient African diaspora whom we must raise from the dead today, praising their presence as we live respectfully and responsibly.

To the many nations of Abraham, Ishmael, Isaac and Jacob, children of our Black Motherland, to our nomadic traders and water bearers crossing still existing boundaries evident for all who would see. To our healers and those ready to be healed.

To our wooly headed visionary cousin, Jesus the Jew, anointed masterful Black superhero, and to the noble magi who found his glory, and to priests, seers and musicians who brought the story. To King David, Psalmist, who premeditated murder, committed adultery and still was beloved of God; and as my Big Ma would say, "Hmmmmm, ain't God wonderful?" To those who would study war no more, reading maps of the world and willing to see with intelligence and not emotion; to the scrutinizing ascendant who recognizes whose presence is the whole bible; and to Buddha, the knotted haired. To the enlightened who no longer need to sing about being washed whiter than snow in order to be somebody.

To those who have no need to puff themselves up at the expense of another's downfall. To our people who are willing to read. And to the queen of the south who has come to hear the word and behold something greater is come. To the first who used to be last and to the up and coming.

To our ancient Hebrew ancestors, spice colored nomads willing to traverse east to west and north to south, and to our stubborn bullheaded ungrateful relatives, wanderers who were forty years (Exodus 16:33; Numbers 16:35) in the desert, and to us, the four hundred year plus ascendants who recognize we are no longer enslaved in the Third World of the United States.

To those of African heritage who care enough to step boldly across nationalities and boundaries, into the twenty first century knowing that we are blessed of God and are willing to do something good for ourselves and our future. Amen. So it is. And so shall it be.

ACKNOWLEDGEMENTS

Each Sister knows the ways in which she has touched
my life. I am thankful God chose you to share an integral part
of yourself with me. Your presence within this universe is
appreciated. Holy Spirit, I know these Sisters are spiritually
and abundantly blessed.

Cheryl Tyrrell; Linda McCullough; Barbara Kay Ratliff;
Michele Shay; Alfreida B.Kenny; Belinda Elliott–Larkin and
Rashida; Bonnie Allen and the Dove; Odehyah "Brandy"
Baht–Israel; Susan L. Taylor– Burns; Yolanda "Yogui" Ackles
and Miss Sunni; Carol J. Strond; Iyanla Van Zant; Dr. Barbara
L. King; Momma Alice Moorer; *ESSENCE* Magazine; Bobbi Jo
Felton; Mrs. Wolfe; Mrs. Madge McGinley; Mrs. Jackson;
Glenna Rowe–Ramsay; Pelar Thompson; Sarah Dash;
Melverue Abraham; Nanna, Evelyn Thompkins–Saunders;
Mom, Ethel Diana Price, who accepted me unconditionally;
Marilyn F. McCullough; Joy Goff; Aunt Willie; Aunt Limmie;
Aunt Red; Aunt Geraldine "Dean" Hale; Aunt Delores "Lois"
Hale; Anna Ruth and Jennifer Jones, who would kill a rock
for Baby June; Valetta Smiley–O'Kelly; Pat Ramsay; Phyllis
Garland; Jean Tice; Phyllis Buford; Gertrude Elizabeth "Lissa"
Sprinkles; Valerie Blakely; Dyanne Fries; Regina E. Brown;
Reverend Marilyn Miller; The Black Fairy; Carol Higgins;
Janice Thompkins–Austin; Stella Jones; Lenore Jett– Boyd;
Ursula M. Portis; Kimberly Renee, Taylor and Ashley, Lynda
Kaye Gatlin; Brenda D. Anderson; Fawn Gatlin and two girls;
to Cindy for birthing Jessica Adelina Gatlin; LaDonna,
Tiffany and A. Michele Gatlin; Dr. Betty Shabazz; Ionia
Dunn–Lee; Terri Williams; Barbara Bush; Cynthia Wade; Joan
Adams Brann; Zenobia Thomas; Margaret Daniels; Darhlene
Dixon; Eisha Mason; Iris Rideau; Patty Coots–Chester; Mabel

Collins; Ornetta Barber–Dickerson; Sister Clara M. Felton
and Sister Wilma Bradford; Mother Ashworth; Donna Allen;
Sister Khadijah Farrakhan; Dorothy Gatlin; Gloria Lily–Holt;
Queen Mother Moore; Harriet Tubman; Soujourner Truth;
Aunt Cassie; Hon. Rosa Parks; Fannie L. Hamer; Barbara
Jordan; Chemin Bernard; Isis and Mary; Rosalyn Ilunga; Anna;
Deborah; Margie Faurier; Dr. Naima Powell; Ernestine
Henning; Virginia "Coe" Woodson; Mary Ann Price; Carolyn
Lewis; Joyce E. Noll; Rickie Byars; Ouida DeSett–Pullin;
Michele "Mikki" Reaves; Dr. Denise Albury; Monica
Woodfox; Evelyn "Butch" Grimes; Dr. Stephanie Lafayette;
Momma Sally; Valerie Wilson–Wesley; L. D. Evans; Audrey
Edwards; Mom Clarke; Bridget Aschenburg; Z. Neal Hurston;
Marrianne Spraggins; Hazel Medina–Matz; Marie Brown;
JoAnn Williams; Dr.Vivian "Yaa" Windley; Toni Morrisson;
Tricia and Tanji Thompkins, Sisters too; Cassandra Nialah;
Angela Oliver; Debra Ainsworth; Maxine Waters; L. Scott
Caldwell; Mertine Moore; Ruby and Joy Tyrrell; Cheryl
Everett; Corliss King; Ann Knox–Johnson; Charolette
Shavers; Alice Walker; Sheila Frazier; Jane Menuez–Santana;
Dafina Moore; Granma Francis Gardner White; Barbara
Anderson who talks back to doubt; Janet Harrell; Monica
Woodfox; Rita Ross; Suzanne DePasse; Janet "JJ" League;
Patricia Thompkins; Arabella Julien; Cyndi James Gossett;
Mary DiBlosi; two Tamus(Oakland & LA); Beverly A. Brown;
Tina Lifford; Canetana Hurd and Jackie Callis; Vicki
Wickham and Nona Hendricks; Jean King; Tanya Hart;
Jaqcueline Trescott; Gloria Rooney; Carol Fries; Marcia Ann
Gillespie; Lorraine Shay; Linda Cannon; Aunt Rebecca and
Aunt Minnie; Patty LaBelle, what a friend we have in Jesus;
and every Sister one and all...

These brothers know the ways in which they have touched
my life. I am thankful God chose you to share an integral part
of yourself in my living experience. Your presence within
this universe is appreciated. Holy Spirit, I believe these brothers
are spiritually and abundantly blessed.

David E. Driver; Gary Noel Hunt; Daddy, Jesse H. Gatlin, Sr,
who adopted me; Max Julien; Bishop C. H. Mason, Founder,
Church of God in Christ; Alex Haley; Kris Keiser; Miles
Davis, for acknowledging my voice; Terry Lee King; Poppa
John Jones; S."Tab" Buford; the Dunagans: the seed father,
Eural Kennedy, uncles T. J. and Charles; Edwin Rideau
Faurier; Lewis Smallwood; Grandaddy, Rev. John H. Hale;
Edward "Ed" Lewis; Al Brandtner; Michael Dyer; Malaney
Hill; Chancellor Williams; Elbert Hamilton Oliver; J. A.
Rogers; Clarence "Larry" Smith; Tom Feelings; Donny
Hathaway, for a friend at midnight; George Anderson,
Waymon L. Jones, Sr. and Waymon L."Louie" Jones, Jr.;
Walter Ainsworth; Kephra Burns; Steven Harrell; Muhzee
Jomo Kenyatta; Melvin Earl Brown; Hon. Percy Sutton; Matt
Robinson, Sr.; Alexander S. Pushkin; Harold Thompkins;
Hon. Marcus Garvey; Hal Scott; Abba, Rabi Ben Ami; Josef
Powell; my great grandfathers; the Nubian; Armando
Santana; James Tyrrell; Kenneth Reynolds; Ruben Cannon,
Sr.; Emmett Till and Michael Donald; Immanuel Ben–Yehuda;
Bro. Thomas Dorsey for Precious Lord; Delbert Edward
Thompkins for that one brief moment of assisting in the
immaculate conception and creation of an atom; Jerry Matz;
Rev. Cecil "Chip" Murray; Phillip Michael Thomas; Chad
James Carstarphen; Daniel Shavers; Darryl Minger; Monte
White; Henry Kinji, Sr.; Orde Coombs; Ramses II; Bishop J.
A. Blake; Attaullah Bashir; Bishop Williams; Uncle Alonzo's
announcement about "the five pounder"; Stanley James;

Hon. Elijah Muhammad; Prof. Timothy Moore; John "Jigs" Saunders; Nasi Shaleak; Alabama Jones, Hales and Moorers; Baba Muktananda; Prince Rashid A. Oluyole; Hon. Medgar Evers; Anthony "Tony" Moses; Dr. Harold Orr; Raymond Giles; Phillip Hart; Kenny Gamble; Apostle Paul, founder of Christianity; Edward Windsor Wright; Thomas "Tommy" Mottola; Jordan (Zankoff) Christopher; Al Bell; Vincent; Rev. Frank Reid; Bishop Solomon Burke; L.V. Beethoven; Million Man March; Rudy Lepinski; Bishop Desmond Tutu; The Old Man, James Black; Sadiki; Count Stovall; Mark Preston; Newman "Poochie" Williams; Raymond Corbin, and Professor James Cleveland; Elder Lemon Butts; Bishop Kelsey; Dad, Elder Willie Price; my brothers: Jerry, Jesse aka "Bucky", who advised me that those who remain have a lifetime to live each day to its fullest, Kelvin and Anthony Gatlin, and Kenneth Dunagan; my nephews, Gregory Wayne Portis II, Kevin Gatlin and Joshua R. Wilborn; Alexandre Dumas; Michael Daoud Carnegie; Bob Law; Dr. Ben Jochananan; Mel Longmire; Brian Behan; Frederick Douglas; Michael Schultz; Prince Asiel; Gary Imhotep Byrd; Dr. John H. Clarke; Hon. Min. Louis Farrakhan; Granpa Ben Hale; Richard "Uncle Bubba" Moorer; Rev. Michael Beckwith for the best peaches; hip slapping quartets; James Daly; Langston Hughes; Charles "Chuckie" Moorer, Jr.; Aaron and Alan McClain; Gene Harris and Marvin Gaye; Bishop C. A. Ashworth; Moses, the Egyptian priest; Dr. M. L. King; Hon. El Hajj Malik El Shabazz; Gerald Jett; Hon. Ronald Brown; Ramon Judkins; Willard Motley; Sinclair Lewis; David Ben Gurion; Mahatma Ghandi; Frank Yerby; Alexander Pushkin; Bishop Vaughn, Miller St. COGIC; and every brother, one and all....

Contents

Introduction

I am First World Wombman of quality
breathed from spiritual substance.
I am God's Creation,
Wombman of distinction.
God's will for me makes a way out of no way.

Sister, read your book during quiet times when you are away from anything you consider to be distracting to your concentration as well as your *consecration*. Each word in a sentence is important. Every word as it is given within a paragraph is important. Savor each word as you would partake of a delicious meal. **Help Yourself!**

Enjoy what you are receiving within the very fiber of your being. Listen as Spirit of God speaks to you in your blood as it flows through your veins into every nerve, cell, and organ of your body.

Spirit speaks to you, Beloved, in your vaginal canal, spine, breasts and thighs. Take pleasure in what you are receiving. Listen and feel God's power in the marrow of your bones, in your navel, your hair, your eyelashes, and your skin. Be comforted knowing that the Divine Spirit is speaking to you inside your throat, in your hands and feet, inside your nostrils, and within your earlobes. Listen as Divine Spirit speaks in your heart and your brain.

Know that God's power is **exact** where you are. Therefore, be in a peaceful state of mind and allow yourself to enjoy these words selected to *inspire, praise, enlighten, elevate, and liberate* you.

DIRECTIVE

After each chapter there will be specific words, **command words,** which must be checked in your dictionary. These words are given so that you can see how they contribute meaning to what you have read. Checking your words represents your acts of faith; and as you know, faith without action is null and void.

Through believing and trusting you will see the manifesting of God's blessings being given for the best of your life and good living.

Spirit requires us to be active participants. **Check Your Words.**

The Open Door

Dearly Beloved Sister,

You are readying to embark upon a most remarkable journey, a magnificent adventure, one that will grant you a new birth and feelings of commitment and joy so fulfilling you will not want to do a thing except revel in the gracefilling good you shall receive.

Spirit speaks is a sacred text given for the healing of nations which had their beginning within the body of God's First World *Wombman*. The words written are for the spiritual, mental, and physical well–being of the Black Wombman wherever she be within universe.

Why, some may ask, must We write a book to and especially for Black Wombman when so many books about spirituality are being written to help all people? Why is a book necessary to inspire Daughters of *First World Diaspora*? Aren't they spiritual enough? Don't they believe in God? Don't they know enough about themselves, their story, their ancestry? Why must they read words emphasizing their importance? Are Black WomenSistersMothersDaughters so special?

Yes you are. *Spirit Speaks to Sisters* is written so that you will **never forget** you were the beginning of First World. And in the ending, which is a new beginning unto itself, you shall be.

This is your entry into your spiritual realm, your place of

spiritual enlightenment. Here is where you are encouraged to become centered within. You are moving beyond illusions and the seeming imperfections of visible/outer world, entering into empowering dominion of the Divine.

Spirit speaks about affirming your personal security. As an ascendant of First World Wombman you are still being black-listed, subjugated and horribly misjudged. Sisters are constantly under attack. Misguided individuals, consumed by their racial and gender prejudices, are giving ugliness new meaning. The media, conservatives, and others zealously manufacture and dispense articles, statistics, and surveys determined to show Black Wombman as the only group still clinging to lower rungs of society's ladders.

Beloved, you have been bearing the burdens of enmity and hostility for too long. Times may appear to be difficult but Spirit is calling for the joyful celebration of Black Wombman.

In this moment, Sister, We want to take you back to your inception. As you read this book you will be revealed as the essence of God's spoken word.

You were breathed into life, made in the likeness of your Creator so that your body would be a living temple, a place of honor for Holy Spirit. You are a loving soul formed from God's heart. **Breathe, Sister, breathe.**

See this book as your living testimony, written by Spirit, allowing you enlightening opportunities to move beyond any barriers impressed within your soul. It is written to liberate you from any thing you may have considered life threatening or emotionally stressful.

Spirit speaks to celebrate you, venerating those who came before you so that you might live, enjoying today and knowing what it means to contribute to your abundance by way of your spiritual works.

You must rise to heights sung and spoken about by the ANCIENT who breathed knowing all things are possible when you believe.

WHAT IS SPIRIT?

Spirit is the Holy and Omnipresent source of God's aliveness. Where God and Spirit of God are concerned, Spirit is life of you. This life allows you the privilege of knowing you are a living being in fleshform of Black Wombman, female human. God is your Originator, Giver of your breathing.

Spirit is like the wind. You can feel and see the evidence of Her presence yet cannot hold Her in your hands. *Spirit is eternal breath*.

Spirit, as you, is and always will be the presence of life to come. Spirit is your powerful life support system, unfailing and always available to encourage you during the most trying of times. Spirit commands you to aspire to greatness.

Divine Spirit is living within your female fleshform. Therefore, it is your duty and responsibility to take heed, paying attention to Spirit who allows you the awe inspiring privilege of knowing your attunement with your soul's source.

Breathe, Beloved. As you are becoming spiritually aware, understand no human has given you breath. Should you choose to trace your aliveness beyond your human mother's womb, you will feel your consciousness originating from God. Sister, make your breathing a celebrating of God and Divine Spirit. You will see life divine being conceived to be birthed as (say your name).

Spirit is your reason for living. Without Her you would be **no** thing, non existing. Therefore, since you are a living being breathing in Divine image of God's loving Spirit, know to whom you owe your life. **Spirit is God. God is Spirit. One and same.**

Spirit is your **Mother** *Nurturer: Mystical.* **Omnipresence.**
Teacher. Healer. Endearing/Endurance. Your Refuge.
Spirit is *Your* **Isness**: *Inspiration/Integrity.* Sacredness.
Nature. Essence. Sanctity. Stability.

THE ANCIENT

Many are mystified by that which is referred to as **The Ancient.** We want to be connected to its existence. And we are; it is one with us; we are inseparable.

We have a sense about things we may have never had a physical experience with. There is a feeling of familiarity, a recognition yet how can we know about things we have never studied or experienced? Have you ever become very adamant about things you know absolutely nothing about, your emotional body vibrating with an intensity that makes your entire being tremble? You have a feeling that goes deeper than emotional self. Somehow you simply know the truth of the matter. Your belief is absolute.

Beloved, this feeling of certainty is your *soul's truth*. It is The Ancient refreshing your recollection, making current in your memory events of the past and bringing into the present things yet to be.

The Ancient is about trusting Spirit. It is about going to the Source who is life eternal. Therefore, eternity is more than an idea. Eternity brings to mind a desire that stimulates us to find who we are, to search for and find our roots. We are moved to seek our origins and to establish our beginnings.

The Ancient is alive today because we are breathing. Souls of our ancestors are alive because we are breathing. Their omnipresence, by virtue of its nature, **is** eternal life. In a sense, we are mystified about ourselves, our livingness, our being and our divine existence. As Spirit ordains: **We are The Ancient.**

·Our soul memories are forever connected....

> *Never Forget!*
> *Always remember and honor your Ancestors!*
> *Be proud of who you are!*
> *Love yourself as you love God!*

SISTERS CHARGE

Sister will heed Divine Spirit's voice and listen to Her words: You will move triumphantly into twenty–first century being honorable, self–respectful and a reverential ascendant of God's First World Creation.

Sisters who elect to dishonor and denigrate themselves shall be blocked and stopped in their self–destructive tracks. God does not choose to lose one soul. What contributions are you giving to family and community? Sisters who continue to ferment in filth mindedness, vile living, and self–imposed squalor are doing wrong unto themselves. What life sharing information are you communicating to children of First World ancestors? Sisters who are being inconsiderate, self–indulgent, and contemptuous of their divine aliveness shall surely perish. What images are you presenting to God's First Nation?

10
▼▼▼

Beloved, We cannot afford to lose a Nation because one Sister is choosing to believe she must abide in a base and/or corrupt lifestyle.

Being divided from God is not spiritual law. How can those of First Creation continue to separate themselves from their Maker? To do so is tantamount to matricide. Think about your heritage, Sister. **Would you murder your mother?**

You are Elect. From blackness came the light. God's breathing moved upon waters in First Mother's womb. Beloved, you are Chosen of God's First World heritage. Spirit is bringing this charge for you to commit to memory:

> I am ascendant of First World Origin.
> I owe my life to the Most High.
> I am born worthy.

Beloved, you must be reminded every moment you are breathing that you are called to higher consciousness. You are chosen to help raise consciousness within your family, your people and your Nation. **You**, Daughter of First World Diaspora, breathe. Whose life is this anyway?

Sister, are you willing to snatch out the root of animosity and self/soul hatred? It is imperative that programming of Nation hostility and distrust be annulled. Collectively, Sisters are directed to come together, to gather and invest in one another, building trust so that each becomes more than participants in segregated societies. Holy Spirit is calling for you to be *creators* and *founders* of Nations, *architects* and *builders* of Divine Kingdoms.

When you were born, a Nation began. Look at yourself, Sister. Look into yourself. Look beyond self. Know your place is highest of high. Committing to **good Leadership** for our new generations is my charge. **Credibility** is my key. My command word: **Education**.

SISTER'S CHARGE
I will not allow any human to destroy my soul.
I honor and cherish my life.
I will not indulge in subterfuge or sabotage
of my family, community or Nation.
I will not allow other's purposeful and negative

hostilities make me hate myself.
I will respect and honor my Sisters'
souls with unconditional love.
I am architect of New World Nations.
I know everything begins with me.
This is my charge: I accept, honor, and cherish it.

Signature: _____

Date: _____ *19*_____

Look at your NationSisterMotherDaughtersGirlsFriends Associates and bear witness to your divine life and spiritual truth. Beloved, be willing to see Divine presence in fleshform of Black Wombman.

ARE YOU READY?

Through absorbing the words of the Spirit contained in this book, you can come into Divine Order, knowing as long as the moon and stars are in the heavens you owe God. You owe respect to this life which breathes itself as you. When you feel and know what your existing is, Sister, you will acknowledge God's very presence as you.

Oh, Beloved, this is your perfect timing, a day for you to move beyond horrid projections of who any human misjudges you to be. Create personal progress by refusing to regress, digress or to allow yourself to be suppressed. This is your time to get rid of anything that has had you chained and bound.

This is your time, Sister. There are no more barriers, real or imagined, which can prevent you from reaching your glory on earth. Now is the time, the perfect timing to contribute all Divine Spirit directs you to complete so that the

12
▼▼▼

future, our future, will become one of magnificence, dedication, and discipline.

It's time to move, Sister, time to **congregate** and **communicate** about achieving for the ascendants who will be standing on the groundwork you have put into place.

Since the advent of your ancestors' enslavement, there has not been one such as you. It is legacy time, Sister, and we have a divine duty to listen as Spirit speaks so that we can do all things with the strengthening powers of God.

We are Daughters of the Most High. Seed, soul and Spirit. We are called to oneness. Heart to heart, soul to soul, and spirit to spirit. Spirit speaks to you about being liberated into unconditional love, liberated to life.

When you have completed this book, you will have read about an unique Wombman, a divine female, a conscientious Daughter who is going about her life excelling in everything she does.

You deserve God's good with abundance.

So there, Beloved. Are you ready? If you are and you have chosen to step through the Open Door, then Spirit says," come! You have a mighty work to fulfill." Spirit says, "come, Dear Sister, come."

Committing to **progress with patience** is your first step. **Faith** is your key! Your command word: **Fearless**.

2

Dreams and Visions

*The Spirit of The Lord is upon me, because She has anointed
me to preach good news to the poor, She has sent me
to proclaim release to the captives and recovering of sight
to the blind, to set at liberty those who are oppressed,
to proclaim the acceptable year of the Lord.*

— LUKE 4:18~19

I have learned to trust the voice of God, knowing what I will hear is truth: It has never led me wrong. I know this distinctive voice to be one that has given strength when I felt discouraged, comfort when I was tiring, and taught me to believe when my faith was being challenged. I learned to listen when Spirit spoke. I know to be obedient when I am hearing its eternal voice to date.

16
▼▼▼

Spirit would warn me about personal choices I was going to make which were not in my best interests. I was not always obedient regarding the warnings, curiously wondering if what I was being told was true. I would proceed with **my** plans because I was adventurous, to say the least.

I would know the truth about my planned experiences but many times I was being hopeful that what I was being shown would not become a reality. I would create doubt because what

I was seeing would sometimes be too difficult for me to handle. Besides, there were some things I wanted to do on my own without interference from Spirit. Therefore, I made what I naively believed to be **my** decisions to step out of the visions.

Much of my rebelling came about because I was tired of being viewed as strange. So much of what was happening I had already known would be. What was my purpose for living in a world that always made me feel ahead of time? And I was. When humans would describe me as being ahead of my time I was not thrilled nor elated. I was frustrated. So I stayed in the mind of leaving a physical world that was so difficult and foreign to what I knew.

My stepping out, as I refer to it at times, was the best thing that could have happened for my life. During times of trauma and frustration, I challenged God and Holy Spirit by questioning Their existing although I always knew of their greater presence with and within me. I knew Divine Spirit was my life force and animator of my being. When I would choose to ignore what I knew was right, the result was inevitable. Spirit was speaking truth.

I began to realize I was being given enough rope to see who is controlling my life. God's unconditional loving and Spirit's protective guidance is evidence of the all knowing wisdom working, simply allowing June to see for herself that Spirit is ever righteous.

THE ONLY LIFE I KNOW

"You can't even die until you complete what you were born to do." Spirit spoke these words when I was suicidal. I wanted to be saved from a world I believed to be too rough, too difficult, so uncaring and terribly disheartening. The reality of the outer world disturbed me; I knew it was not truth. I was always in battles, going to war within regarding things I knew did not have to be. The revelations in my dreams and visions seemed to be overpowering me. I wanted release.

I watched serious and eventful moments come then go and I'd cry out to God: "Send me something to help with these dreams and visions I see. I need strength!" Inevitably Spirit, **the only life I know,** becomes my Comforter allowing me the privilege of knowing I am never without strengthening love and courage. My distressful situations were educational times, moments of training. With each trauma I have had to overcome, I became stronger and more confident with Spirit's comforting words: "Take heart. Be still and know!"

There were times when my life could only be described as very, very painful. I did not like having visions or having to deal with human's delusions of what they presumed my life was about. Much of my hurt resulted from having to deal with individuals who had misconceptions about what they believed my abilities to be.

At age three I was proclaimed a prophetic child by the saints in The Church Of God In Christ. I had the **gifts** of vision and healing. My great–aunt Limmie told me I was born with the veil. She said I had the "knowing power, just like your grandmother and your mother." It is in our lineage.

In ancient times Africans recognized a child born with the· sight. It was considered a blessing and it was an honor for the family, village, and community.

Today, seeing into the unseen and calling it forth frightens most humans and because of their fears I have, at times, been condemned, referred to as satanic or evil. Humans tend to misjudge what they know nothing about; their fear of anything they deem supernatural dredges up all sorts of unseemly actions.

My childhood experiences were quite extraordinary. I knew the definition of being ostracized personally because of my ability to see events before they actually happened. Knowing how people feel and think about you can be a heavy burden for a child. Pretending as if I was unaware was even heavier. I learned the diplomacy of not speaking about what Spirit had revealed. My silence could be uncomfortable for humans who wanted to know yet feared asking. However, when a healing or a blessing was needed, some conveniently forgot how they contributed to the mistreatment and disapproval of my existence.

As an adult I was still being bombarded by many humans who had no inkling of how God and Holy Spirit worked with me. I have been accused of being everything but a child of God. So many of these judgements originated from people who had read about or seen me on television. For years I cried; I tried to find the strength to take my life. I wanted to get out of the world as I knew it. I asked, "Lord, please let me die!"

It was difficult for me to handle the slightest disappointments. Again, I was pretending not to know how people were looking at me. I could sense immediately what was going on with them. I knew when humans were attempting to hide their thoughts, fearing I would know about their lives or what they may have done or were doing. I was as uncomfortable as they were.

It is not my life intention to pry into anyone's private times. I don't have to. When Spirit decides I must know what is going on, privacy becomes a nonexisting thing. God and Holy Spirit don't care about June's privacy. When it is life saving time the only reality is helping a person to live.

It is interesting for me when I see humans who have contributed to some of my most uncomfortable moments. They never knew how difficult it was for me. I look at them with the natural eye, and I see with my knowing how they are hopeful I have forgotten the pain and turmoil they brought into my life. I will never forget. A life saving rule Spirit revealed to me: Do not hold grudges, do not harbor animosity and, most of all, remember who I am. This is the reality of my life. I did not choose this, I was predestined to be born Black and female with paranormal abilities.

SPIRIT TAUGHT ME

Holy Spirit comes to me during my sleep or when I am awake. I can be having conversation, dining, or in a crowd of ten thousand. Anytime the Lord wanted to give me words and visions, They would bring them. I receive them. I cannot run away. There is no where I can hide.

When asked where did I learn to do the things I do, my response is, "Spirit taught me!" It is the only source helping me to come through some of the most difficult times of my living by simply saying: "You can handle this because you have to. You know how!"

When I was a child, I was told I am born to help my people. When I was eleven years of age, I asked God, "please don't let me leave this earth until I see something good happening for my people." I will never forget these words. Never. Every experience I was given contributed to my ability to fulfill my God given mission. Spirit was making me stronger, more dedicated and more determined to inspire African ascendants to reclaim our spiritual heritage and represent God on earth.

Through my pain, my frustration and every deed done to me, kind and unkind, I keep on keeping on. Every moment I wanted to get away from my people's hurting, our seeming eternal grieving. I cannot. I am still here and I am still on purpose, assisting in our determined steps to return to the only life we know, Spirit. This life breathes itself within our blood, allowing us the opportunities of knowing there is something greater surrounding and within us, Spirit. I am knowing every vision, every dream and all Holy Spirit's words come to reveal we can become greater.

God's Spirit speaks allowing me the honor of declaring those things which are to be. And when we listen, obediently following through, everything works for our good. I know because They do not cease to show me whatever is required for my life's journey.

It has not mattered how despondent I became nor did it matter if I was attempting to run from God's will. I can never get away from my birthright. God's aliveness is breathing within my skin. It is not my sight I am believing with. I am given the spiritual I of God's living sight which is the inner visible and it becomes the only life I know.

My whole being is breathing God's will.
Everything you are Spirit Is.
And everywhere you be, Spirit lives.

LET SPIRIT HAVE ITS WAY

And you must again prophesy about many nations, cultures, and governments...

— REVELATIONS 10:11

Bleeding women have the life of God and this makes us not common beings but exceptional life givers. We have the life source of God flowing through our bodies and this is to give living proof of a greater power which commands life to be born.

We are birthed into this world to be spiritual nurturers for one another.

As Spirit speaks to date, Sisters, I know I am given encouraging words for all of us. I have given much time in thought regarding what to say to my Sisters. Spirit advised that it is not my words but the soul from which I write. Open my heart and let Spirit have its way.

Our people are in turmoil, lashing out violently and attempting to annihilate God's First World Creations from the earth. Black people are lynching, castrating and destroying our own by violent actions and words.

I wanted to get away from this world, from everything I saw and knew but God had a greater work for me to complete. In the Bible there is a scripture which reads: "When The Spirit of truth comes it will guide you into all the truth; for it will not speak on its own authority but whatever it hears it will speak and declare unto you those things which are to come." (John 16:13)

Who would want this duty? Surely not I. It is God's will being done with my life. I would not be a living being in flesh-form of female human, a child of the First World inception, if it were not the will of my God. So here I be, giving written words as Spirit speaks.

22
▼▼▼

I totally relate to the words attributed to the Prophet Isaiah: "The Lord has given me the tongue of those who are taught, that I may know how to sustain with a word anyone who is weary. Morning by morning my ear is awakened to hear as those who are taught. The Lord has opened my ear and I am no longer rebellious. I turn not away." (Isaiah 50:4–5)

I know I could never cease believing because God has done mighty works for me, revealing things that are yet to be. All the things I have been given to see tells me we shall be those ascendants God determined we had to become **before we were born.**

Loving the Lord is the only life I know. Human misjudgment has not prevented what Holy Spirit declares through me. Nothing has stopped the will of God from working in my life. I love myself and the life presence that I am as a Black Wombman. I have come to accept who I be and everything about me is special and unique unto God, *as you are*, Beloved Sister. We are daughters of the Most High.

Love is healing. Holy Spirit taught me to see beyond human frailties and to know love for the wholeness of my life. I have had to pray for tolerance and patience; I know the meaning of praying for those who misuse and abuse. Despite my aching, I am that place of healing. For my soul's sake, I know love for humanity to be greater.

I was taught to believe in my *knowing* abilities by Spirit because everything revealed came to be. This was the only proof necessary for me to understand the plan was bigger than the natural eye could see.

As I live, Holy Spirit gives me solid and sensible answers. No words, actions or attitudes can stop my dreams and visions. My world is the inner reality which allows me to move beyond human misconceptions. Painful words, the mental and physical abuse I endured, and whatever human actions I have experienced, I am thankful because they served to make me stronger.

Lord, I am grateful for every small thing: my joys and disappointments, my successes, and every hurt or pain I thought too mighty for me to deal with.

I am thankful daily because I am knowing that just as I came through my difficult times, *so can we all.*

I say, **"Thank you"** to God and Divine Spirit for the gifts of healing, prophetic visions and dreams. There is no clearer sight than to be able to see Your loving and divine meaning. Thank you God and Holy Spirit for giving me the most loving life I know. I knew I was given a special place of spiritual security where no thing could harm me, *a place where visions still have a voice.*

> *Without Spirit we are nothing.*
> *With It as our Being we are all things.*
> *We are Daughters of the Most High.*

3

Spiritual Fitness

I know I be and will become all
Holy Spirit reveals for Me.

Good life, Sister. Rise and shine. Are you ready to raise, praise and celebrate your life? Spiritual fitness is your daily exaltation program inspiring you to get in shape spiritually, mentally and physically. Getting attuned within and creating a comfortable program for improving your life and the physical body helps to keep you feeling good about yourself.

Spirit speaks to you about *exercising* and *exorcising*, receiving good for body and releasing any and all negativity destructive to your being. Sister, a change is taking place. It's obvious you are now determined to transform your life.

A newly defined Sister needs to be celebrated. Therefore, spiritual fitness is your positive plan, essential for maintaining, strengthening, healing, toning and uplifting both your inner and outer body. Your plan, your individualized spiritual fitness program, requires exercise and daily devotion consisting of prayer, praise, meditation and/or quiet time.

BRAIN WASHING

What are you allowing to come into your brain? Is your

brain inviting and receiving ugly, hostile images and impressions? What negative messiness is living there? Is this a place where mold is growing? Is your consciousness generating diseased thinking? Your brain can no longer tolerate unhealthy language, or can it? Whose brain is this anyway?

Get up, lets talk. What is the first thing you're hearing? Are you listening to words that are powerfilling or are you replaying negative programming, focusing on tapes continuously describing everything that has gone wrong, could be and is probably going to be wrong? Is it easier to focus on all the bad stuff than it is to workout? If your answer is yes, then it is time to get impersonal: Deprogramming. Brain washing. No more endearing negatives; no more holding them closer than hands and feet simply because of habit.

Stop clouding your head with foul thoughts. Self ridiculing thoughts no longer require your brain as a favorite vacation space. When was your last brain washing? If your answer is confirming more than a week ago, it's your time for brain drain. It's time to tone that muscle, Sister.

Wake up, Beloved. Look at the aliveness of Divine Spirit. Are you seeing your *place of veneration*: everything good, pure and righteous about you? Take this quiet moment and look at God's face, Beloved. Study *your* face. Now move beyond eyes. Who do you see? If you begin to feel dizzy, a little bit off balance, this is good. It's meaningful. Breathe, Beloved. Breathe.

Don't fear anything you may hear coming into your brain. Keep looking. Now relax. Allow body to slowly hear sound of her breathing. Can you hear her breath? It's listening for you! This is healing time.

Any pictures, images, thoughts, ideas or impressions seemingly negative, let them flow. They are leaving anyway. Unwanted and unwelcome, they will flee from your inner sanctuary. Look at them messes, getting out any way they can. Every nook and cranny of brain is being readied for cleansing. Take your time; be at ease. Can you picture peacefulness within yourself? Excellent.

This may be work for some Sisters, but with Holy Spirit doing the guidance here, you are guaranteed a new thought processing machine. Work with Spirit, Sister. Spirit is working within you. She is your trainer. The brain is muscle. We're walking you through this; and you know how much patience is required to establish good muscle tone, don't you? And you know how to be relaxed, not rushed, don't you? Veneration is restorative. **Help Yourself!**

How are you feeling, Sister? Calmer? Tired, but more relieved? Well, keep on looking. *Keep looking within.* See that brain tissue, a grayish mass, many crevice like areas, some lumpiness, a few bumps? Are there any craters, small holes that you have attempted to fill with messes? Okay, this is tool time. Visualize any beautiful, well made surgical tool or other instrument, perhaps a scalpel, drill, chisel, shovel, pick, rake, hammer, hose or even dental floss, whatever you work best with. Enter into your memory bank where much of the residue of negative emotional activity is hiding, determined to keep holding on, hoping that perhaps someday you may want to reclaim the messes for personal insecurity time. Step into that brain mass like the authority you are and work that muscle. See you scraping, scrubbing, brushing, spraying, showering. Is suction necessary, Sister? Whatever is required by Spirit to do it, use it. Get that stuff out *now.* **Help Yourself!**

We recommend that you do your brain washing daily because the slightest bit of cruddy thinking is harmful to Beloved's whole being. Sister has no time to be a deadhead; you are not a First World ascendant choosing to be a place for waste; you are not a home for nonstimulating information. A healthy brain can be an active and fertile instrument contributing to longer life. Your healthy days on earth will be increased; desires for dysfunctional living will cease.

Ahhhh, Sister is performing an astronomical work washing and cleaning her brain. Flex and stretch. Your muscle tone is sharp. Every cell, neuron, and nerve ending is healing perfectly. See brain restored, receptive to God's good works. See brain shining and lucid. Visualize a resplendent aura surrounding your head. Brain luminous, complimenting Beloved's wonderful accomplishments. Yes, confidence becomes you.

Am I ready to meet new and fascinating individuals? Knowing that an active brain is stimulated by positive and intellectually inspiring individuals, am I ready to communicate intelligently with other Sisters who are willing to share creatively inspiring information?

WRITING OFF
Today I am canceling mess.
Getting rid of confusion that's been hanging around like
cobwebs on my ceiling.
I'm releasing my soul from tiredness and antiquated
unmeaningful crap.
Stepping out of the traps that have long been rusted.
I'm doing like some companies when they reorganize:
They forgive human debts, write off losses and establish credit
for themselves. The way things ought to be.
There are some things that simply need to be written off.
Some people too.
No need, rhyme nor reason to keep holding onto stuff that is
over, finished and done.

Holding on as if the sorrow is lifesaving.
Holding on as if it's security, whining, complaining, on a search
and recovery mission just to find someone who would be
willing to listen to the same old...
Oh,
Oh,
I am writing off misery.
I am writing off my self, erasing nonchalance, allowing
opportunities of goodness to flow to me.
I want the righteous life I know is due me.
I've touched life's greatness and I'm determined to hold on.
Anything in my way I'm writing off.
It's too easy to collect dust and grime, too easy to let dirt build
a mound around my feet.
I've seen the results.
All it does is take up time cleansing with real tears.
Today I begin clearing away all that is messy: got to be fixin'
and puttin' new coats on that which is requiring painting.
I'm an interior designer (smile).
I'm writing off trendy things, hanging on to what I know
is everlasting: Peace, tranquil moments of importance, and love.
I don't need interruptions nor interruptive individuals,
no things of intrusion.
I'm writing off any, everything I want to when
it's unsuitable.

32
▼▼▼

Signature:_____

POWER TALKING

A healthy brain is an active and fertile
instrument contributing to longer life.

Your healthy days on earth will be increased,
desires for dysfunctional living will cease.

Let us move on to **power talking**, stimulating words for you and your body. As soon as Spirit awakens you, give thanks to God for your breathing. For example: *Thank You God for breathing your life as me.*

Divine Spirit speaks of making personal declarations by saying something nice to yourself. Don't be afraid to out talk self. In other words, where negative programming existed (note: past tense "existed") know you can reach a harmonious understanding within rather than tearing yourself apart for whatever reasons.

Personal putdowns are never imperative. How many times have you awakened hearing negative tapes replaying declarations making you ill equipped to make it through the day? Another one of those hazy days, moments where body is totally uncoordinated with **mind** and being blatant in its determination to ignore Spirit. Don't want to do a thing and **no** thing can make it move.

Sister, this is such a messy situation. It is not fun fighting lethargy resulting from negative programming. You've got to work at it. Got to work the listless feelings out and get that energy going, Beloved. Don't be afraid to out talk self.

Power talking requires concentration and consecrating from within. Stop relying on outer world interruptions, any pacifying things preventing you from moving through your day peacefully and energetically. Sister, Divine Spirit requests your presence without any pill popping, caffeine ingesting and external pick me ups. Get up, Daughter. All the empathy in this universe will not make you feel better about your life until you see what is necessary for you to express your aliveness. Self talking, power talking, can be positive. And where flesh is weakening, Spirit in all ways is willing.

Are you getting up, Sister? All right, Beloved. Lets get busy. Deep breathing gets the heart rate going. Talk yourself upwards:

> *I am (Declare your name).*
> *I am alive.*
> *I am a living loving creative Sister.*
> *Every breath I make returns love to God.*

Even while at work, deep breathing and saying something nice to yourself will reenergize you. Go into that sacred space where Divine Spirit is ever present and out talk anything burdensome or attempting to wear you down. Run into your loving sanctuary and get a dose of heavenly vitamins. *Spirit gives good love, Sister.* You know this. Look at who is emerging you, Daughter. It's difficult getting away from having to be in shape spiritually isn't it?

Getting that sweet sensing about you, Beloved? Power talking makes you want to do something good for your body, doesn't it? What words of enthusiasm and strength are you hearing Spirit speak? Say them aloud. Say them as you are moving throughout your living space. Know Divine Spirit sees you as Her living room. Talk for your life, Beloved. There is every good thing going for you when you are taking yourself in confidence. Declare service to you, words that speak good about you. Talk that power influencing grace throughout your body. Compliment you, Sister. Is there a better way to begin your life?

34
▼▼▼

> *God's brilliance is illuminating my life.*
> *My aliveness is required to do excellent*
> *works for God.*

MEDITATION AND QUIET TIME

See quietness as your friend.
Hear Spirit speaking for your life.

Meditation is inner workout, strengthening and toning mental body, cleansing, nurturing, renewing and extending vitality to you.

You are meditating, aren't you? Didn't you fix a special space for yourself, quiet and away from intrusion? Coming this far means you surely are listening to that ever present voice that has directed you to this point.

Oh, Beloved, give you credit for knowing you have not had to await some miraculous moments to know you are doing right about your life. You are validated simply because you are seeking within during quiet moments, listening and knowing you can understand _____(your name). Spirit is speaking about spirituality being your foundation. You come to know this when you meditate.

When you look into your mirror, Beloved, do you appreciate who you see? Or do you cringe? Matters not! Spirit requests that you go into that inner mirror, seeing God's reflection, seeing a loving inner–vision and be still. Quietly now, Sister, release your quest for outer approval. Relax, sensing the overall peace of Divine Spirit's appreciation.

Still yourself from within. No matter what is going on outside, no matter what business needs your immediate attention, no matter whose problems seem bigger than your personal private complimentary time...No thing matters more than you because you are a matter requiring God's immediate attention. You are coming within to see beauty being reflected through God's **I**.

In this stillness, this quiet space where loving is eternally appropriate, in this serene environment where human misjudging is nonexisting, inside the unlimited and unrestricted calmness, you are seeing loving. You are witnessing self being given every consideration possible so that you understand your ability to transform your life. Within you God's queendom is; within you are many mansions. You always have a place to be. You are, always have been, and will forever live as a Wombman unique in God's vision.

Here you are, Beloved, *more than an image and greater than a human reflection*. What you are viewing within is your soul's truth. Seeing truth about you is a huge part of spiritual fitness. Seeing and bearing witness to who you are becoming and more than willing to be, believing and knowing you will achieve all you are being given to see, is definitely your step within the righteous direction.

Yes, We say, "the righteous direction" because in your stillness the consoling you seek is always forthcoming. Fear not, Beloved. Seek and you will see exactly who your God is creating you to be. You can hear Spirit speaking from your soul. You can hear in the stillness all the words Divine and Loving Spirit gives so that you may proceed through your days and nights as one who is new and has not an iota of consternation regarding her precious life. The mirror speaks what it knows is absolute truth when one is silent enough to see what is coming forth.

Be still and know you, Beloved.

Beloved Sister, ascendant of First World Creation and Daughter of Original Diaspora, be confident, assured, and secure in knowing all you seek about you can be found within.

Move into that special inner sanctuary and listen to Divine Spirit as you see your life unfolding. **Trust. Believe. Be an active doer and achieve.**

By this time you are very much in sync with you. Sister knows who she is and thoroughly enjoys seeing more about herself. Surpassing any restrictive limitations is no longer a priority because you, Beloved, are in the consciousness of accomplishing. You know what your inner communing offers. You know saying something nice to and about you revs you up; you know what it is to quiet yourself.

> *I go within and I see my life.*
> *I know I BE when I greet myself.*
> *I know I BE and will become all*
> *that Holy Spirit reveals for me.*

BODY WORK

Spirit speaks about being spiritually fit every moment you are breathing. As you are learning to enjoy your personal quiet times and reveling in your newly creative environment, then you also know how important it is for you to get some physical exercising going. All that good talking empowering body and mind is generating vital information into your computer brain. Well, it's time to release procrastination and make something happen. Body, body, body physical, we've got to get a move on.

Before you begin your celebrating, Sister, be sure you consult with your physician regarding your health consciousness. If you already have a personal trainer or are enrolled in a fitness center, this is wonderful. You've only just begun. It is important to know your body's capabilities; however, the support given here will assist you so that you will work according to what

37
▼▼▼

your body can handle. Do not place unnecessary pressure or burden yourself by attempting to accomplish, too quickly, goals that are unrealistic. "Problems" held in check for years must be worked out gradually with patience. **Do not measure your progress by another's steps. Work lovingly with you!**

What about high stepping, Sister? Walking with music or a steady paced stroll, having your own rhythmic melodies being created each step you're making. Some Sisters make their own music, don't you? If your response is a resounding *yes* then lets get it on. Lets start. Don't stop. Refuse to let anything, anyone, **no** thing block your progress to date. Everything is about power. And power contributes to progress especially when First World ascendant knows how many have walked for her life. Many are coming because you have walked, Sister, so keep a steady pace for your life's time. Breathe, Beloved, breathe.

Squatting, bending, jumping and running. These workouts can be done in early morning, afternoons and evenings. What about work? What about it? Environment does not have to prevent you from catching a few good moves. Ceiling to toe reaches, about ten in a place where you feel comfortable can do a lot to reenergize you when you're getting a tired, listless feeling.

Often when you begin to feel the beneficial results of your workouts you want to shout, jump and dance. Dancing is a spontaneous way to express yourself, no lessons necessary. Just go with the flow and let yourself move. Go, Sister. Move that body and listen to your inner rhythms. That heartbeat is the drum which lets you know you're moving to your own sound. Workout, Sister. Dance. Release. Move. Be spontaneity. Be satisfying for yourself, Beloved, not looking for outer satisfaction to keep you feeling fine about your life. Doesn't it feel good to feel good about you?

Sister, being spiritually, mentally and physically attuned with Divine Spirit, moving to the energetic rhythms of your heart, listening during your quiet time and hearing with understanding all Spirit speaks lets you know life is about you. Surrounding you. Thank you, Divine Spirit, for loving me to life.

IN TOUCH AND IN TUNE

Spiritual fitness—brain washing, power talking, meditating and body work—what has any of these to do with rising and shining, raising and celebrating Sister's aliveness? Doing all that you can to accomplish positive results for inner and outer body *workout* insures your well being. You will see how good you feel. Dancing, walking, talking, singing, praying, praising and celebrating God's life as yours keeps you moving in oneness with Holy Spirit. *A First World Daughter works out while staying in tune and in touch with her life.*

Quick fixes don't work. Spirit is not a temporary prescriptive nor does it support lackadaisical attitudes. When Spirit moves you got to show some sign. Giving time to your inner support sustains you in the external world. You feel you can accomplish anything. You start living the awareness that all things are possible unto you. This is spiritual fitness too? Absolutely. Everything having to do with you requires aliveness of God to be well maintained, focused with faith, showing evidence and proof of your well being and being willing to talk about who gives you power.

Did you meditate yesterday, Beloved? Are you meditating today? Are you giving regenerative moments to yourself tonight? What about now? Do you have anything better to do for you, right here and now, than savor a few brief moments with Spirit?

Breathe, Child, breathe. And know that Divine Spirit is assisting you in erasing self–neglect resulting from holding onto negatives. Release any consternation and uncertainties about your ability to accept the impossible. Your God is manifestor of your good. Let go of insecurities you are protectively guarding. For Beloved, all things rightful are possible. God's invisible protection is more powerful than your worries or concerns. Throw the canceling statement, "its unbelievable!" from your vocabulary.

Precious Sister, you can make a difference with self discipline, determination and willingness to be a blessing. You are to be treasured, held in high esteem and revered. This veneration begins with you. Breathe this knowingness, Daughter. Breathe.

However you find comfort when reaching your specific goals for maintaining the most positive results for your precious life, simply **be** in All knowing of God's mighty Mind. You will to be doing God's Will and whatever you seek in righteousness shall be done unto you. Your good will come. Be an active participant, see with clarity, and divine sight of Holy Spirit will always guide you. Beloved, committing to **spiritual living** is your second step. **Dedication** is your key! Your command word: **Discipline**.

Beauty

From the darkness came the light
Black is beautiful all ways.

Sister, when you look into the mirror who do you see? Do you find yourself making misjudgments about your appearance based upon concepts of beauty which have nothing to do with you or your culture? Are you allowing your physical attributes to distort your thoughts about what beauty is? Are you disturbed, for any reason, about not seeing your image extolled as lovely? Are you constantly in amazement when someone gives you a compliment, especially when you're not feeling good about yourself?

These questions are given for your personal introspection and your answers determine exactly how you envision your presence for life. If you do not love the one you are seeing then you already know it is time for transformation, don't you?

Surrendering to fantasies and illusions of "classical" beauty founded in European consciousness will only serve to keep Sister full with sadness. You will be mentally blue from what you believe perfection is, depressed because of what you think you must look like in order to be a lovelier presence in the world.

First World Creation, the measuring of your life, your desires to be validated by standards that have zero to do with you, creates continual feelings of limitation, lack of character, and no self—esteem.

You are the one who must break the ties of self—hatred. Release your life from the burdensome weight of misshapen societal concepts of beauty: media, marketing and advertising ideals of European charm and loveliness. This idolization of whiteness and the exclusion of Black aesthetics keep First World Daughters mired in cosmetic dysfunction.

Beloved, you are more than a straw in the wind. By now you should know that whichever way fashion trends blow, you could be in or out. When you become prey to misconceptions and disparaging words or any unflattering descriptions written to further the cause of your nonvisibility in any form of media, recognize and know where the real insecurity lies. And that's exactly what it is, **lies**.

There have been lies and more lies written and spoken about your beauty, your hair textures and especially your vibrant skin tones which are evident, internationally, in a multiplicity of beautiful shades and hues. Black Wombman, your complexions range from the bluish black of night to reddish brown, tan, and lighter yellows, palest white and albino.

Touch your skin, Beloved. It is a living organism. Spirit is breathing within your skin as female human. Black Wombman, God created your beauty filled temple for Divine Spirit to dwell within.

SHADES AND HUES

Sisters must stop denouncing other Sisters because of skin color. This is ugly thinking created from envy; it is insanity derived from self—hating ignorance. Where is the spiritual rule written which states that lighter and paler skin automatically makes a Sister wiser, more attractive and greatly desirable? Where is the spiritual law established making darker complexioned Sisters less attractive and undesirable?

Your complexion was given to you by God. It is not a fading moment which comes and goes in a flash. It is not a temporary thing. Sisters must run, climb, hop, jump, or whatever to escape the ugliness thinking which has made so many Sisters cringe. Breathe, Daughter. Breathe. Never Forget: **There are individuals burning themselves to death to achieve what you are birthed to wear majestically.**

> *I Rejoice, praising and celebrating my body.*
> *Oh, how I Rejoice for being me.*
> *I Rejoice, praising my being.*
> *I am alive!*

I celebrate my skin (Sign your name on dotted line)
I Am:_____

HAIR

Spirit speaks to Daughters of First World Diaspora about being enslaved to hair. Are you living for hair? Have you been loved or unloved because of hair? Are you feeling fearful about having hair today and none tomorrow? Are you looking askance at other women's silken tresses thinking about your lack of and wanting more? Would Beloved dare enslave herself to rude, hard to handle and unmanageable hair?

Do you consciously ignore loving your hair just the way it is? Are you a true heiress loving being God's glory or are you living expressly to promote other cultural extensions of beauty? What message is First World Daughter sending to her baby girls? Are divine ascendants being groomed, made to feel ashamed if they don't have long luminous locks? Would you invite future ascendants into your world only to have them believe they are unworthy of honor unless they can swing hair from side to side? How many Sisters do you know who can truthfully lower their head to receive one hundred shining strokes? What are you misusing for your head, Beloved? Is this plus conditioning or negative thinking? Where is your power, Sister?

A First World Daughter knows hair is not crowning glory. Divine Spirit is your radiance. You should know it doesn't matter whether you are headed full with hair, close cropped, braided, straightened, twisted long, short or locked. It is the Spirit in your attitude which allows Beloved's beauty to shine. God is caring about whole souls, not disjointed Sisters caught up in external knots.

What beauty books are you reading and what contribution are they making to this less than thinking? Deal with Spirit's interpretation when She speaks to you about beauty. She's talking about surpassing slights and rallying forth for a unique creation. **You**. She's speaking to you about your life and God's love. She is speaking to your soul, Sister. Well, for some of you this can be a hair raising experience.

47
▼▼▼

> *I Rejoice, praising and celebrating my body.*
> *Oh, how I Rejoice for being me.*
> *I Rejoice, praising my being.*
> *I am alive!*

I celebrate my hair (Sign your name on dotted line)
I Am:_____

PRAISING MY BODY

Sisters' bodies are designed in many beautiful shapes: tall and thin, short and small, bodies medium, heavy and petite. Stacked stallions built like brick houses. Skinny Sisters, some long and lean like reeds or papyrus. We also have our big beautiful Daughters, grand and well rounded, who are counted among our more generously endowed.

We speak of the First World *inheritors* known for those poetically rapturous behinds/buttes/derrieres. Some of society's less fortunate describe Sister's round rumps as too wide to skate with, too huge to race beside and too high to get over. Research and find that European women, Victorians, were wearing bustles to achieve these renown behinds.

Sisters' blessings are being sought after worldwide. Big lips, for example, are now described as "full," sensual, and tantalizing. When it comes time for rediscovering these attributes of Blackness, *nature all* to you, Beloved, all descriptions are changed. Surely the jealousies are obvious. Envy is not becoming although it is evident. And envy is enlightening especially when Sister realizes the spiritual truth about God's divine presence: You.

New fashion amendments are rewritten overnight and constitutions for beauty are amended, made to fit those who are running hither and yon to find a loveliness much maligned and previously overlooked. And fashion designers are yet calling you forth.

"I want to be like Sister." Even the most impotent imitation, at its best, is some form of flattery, Beloved. Take a look at yourself and see who a true beauty is.

As First World Creation: **Do not wish nor yearn to be anyone other than your God self**. Your magnificence is extolled in song, poetry and epics; it is whispered about. The influence of the African Wombman is being carried over to date because you are alive, Sister. Take a God look at your presence and believe! Beauty is in the mind of loving Sister's life.

> *I Rejoice, praising and celebrating my body.*
> *Oh, how I Rejoice for being me.*
> *I Rejoice, praising my being.*
> *I am alive!*

I celebrate my body (Sign your name on dotted line)
I Am:_____

THE ESSENCE OF LOVELINESS

Standards of beauty are no longer the sole property of the European. Look at yourself. Spirit is breathing Her beauty filled presence as you. You are First World's essence of loveliness. Impress this into your consciousness.

Sister is a First World ascendant, birthed to rise, not go down. You are not descending. You come from a lineage of hope not hopelessness. It's time to shed all lackluster views, Beloved, It's time to shine your illustrious lights for all the worlds to see. Breathe, beautiful Wombman. Breathe.

Committing to **celebrating my life** is my third step. **Compassion** is my key. Your command word: **Wisdom**.
And never forget:

> *From the darkness came the light*
> *Black is beautiful all ways.*

5

Loving Works

I am First Creation.
My whole being is a proclamation for
life, liberty and owning my happiness.

S ister is subject to many emotional experiences and vulnerable to numerous influences which can cause conflicting actions, making her feel emotionally off balance and insecure. So much of what you encounter comes as a result of relationships with those whom you love. These humans seem to know which buttons to push. Sometimes you feel they simply want to mess up your day. Why? Simply because they are breathing. What inconsiderate people! Selfish, aren't they?

Beloved, affirming love is truly your answer. You are allowed to **Help Yourself**, making love a personal contribution to yourself. Divine Spirit speaks about being considerate of you, commanding you to let your love be conspicuous. *Loving Works is about love.* Love does not cast stones, misjudge or blame. Do you know what love is, Sister?

52
▼▼▼

Now is your time to **Help Yourself** by declaring your Loving Works:

My Love is empowering, understanding and patient.
Love is compassion.
Love is assurance. Love looks over, passing beyond faults,
frailties and seeming failures.
Love is uplifting. Love is praising.
Love is celebrating my life.
Love is fulfilling. Love is generosity.
Love looks over, is caring. Love is giving solace.
Love nurtures. Love is abundance.
Love keeps promises.
Love protects and sustains, endures and remains love.
No matter the circumstances, love rescues.
Love smiles. Love brings laughter,
tears and good times during sorrow.
My love reverberates and liberates.
My love is never stifling.
Love is warm, giving comfort.
Love is sustenance, thirst quenching.
Love is food.
Love is youth in elder times.
In times like these love is guidance.
My Sister love is apparent when no parent is available.
In darkness my love is light.
With peace my love abides.
When hours are long and time passes slowly, my loving works.
I help my life with love!
I bring my loving works to life!

Spirit is defining you, Beloved, commanding you to honor
your life as an exemplary Wombman. Acknowledge yourself as
an original interpretation of spiritual beauty. Believe this: **Self
knowledge is beautifying.** It may seem a heavy responsibili-

ty for some of you who have become regulars at proclaiming personal imperfections, but every Sister must be ready to step out of self defacing thinking. You are more than a cosmetically enhanced female human. There's nothing like the real thing, Beloved. After all, when everything is taken off what remains is true Sister. *God's First Creation.*

Sister is not a lost female, lonely and unloved. First World Wombman has been entrenched too long in unrefined definitions established by humans who are unkind, abusive and acting in disrespectful ways. It has not been suggested, commanded, demanded, or requested that you place Spirit's breathing in jeopardy by hanging onto the fringes of self destruction. You are living evidence of First Wombman's existence. *Never allow past deeds to cover you forever with guilt and suppression.* If you do this you are creating continual victimhood, thereby endangering the aliveness of God: You.

There is no prerequisite establishing that you are to sacrifice your life in order to live good. The wonderfilling nature of God is your loving protective Spirit, aliveness breathing itself as you this very moment. This aliveness is powerful, powerfilling and victorious. You are not given this holy breath to cower in fear of any human. You are not breathing a spirit of timidness, attempting to hide behind illusions or facades of fright. It is your time to be fearless, standing forth, making your life a statement of inner security. You know things of the flesh pass away, Sister, but Holy Spirit's victories are eternal. This is your time to make your living memorable.

Look at yourself. Here you are ready to stake your claim, knowing victory is absolute where you are. Spirit is speaking to you about being triumphant, a divine life force, a light which man nor woman can put out. Take a long look at the temple in which God's aliveness is breathing. Do you see any bruises, burns, or markings resulting from physical abuse? Are there remnants of mental scars causing you daily pain? How have you handled lies, personal misjudgments? What about shameful smearing, the denigrating of your name? Don't be afraid to acknowledge everything about your life including rattling those bones in the closet. This is Sister's **spiritual inventory**.

Beloved, look at what Spirit is telling you. Have you disrespected your flesh by committing any foul or harmful deeds to yourself? Have you done damage to your life by allowing anyone to invade your loving place? Take time to see who is coming to you with negative words, thoughts and ideas. Breathe, Sister, breathe.

Spirit is referring to abuse: mental, physical or sexual. Have you subjected yourself to any form of violence, purposeful actions of harm to your sacred space? Is your life being disregarded? Has anyone negated your spiritual anointing? Is God's aliveness being compromised in any manner?

Is this sounding familiar to you, Beloved? If your response is yes to any of these questions, this is your time to request help. **Trust Holy Spirit to guide you.** It's time to go within to receive Divine Guidance.

Breathe, Dear Heart. Breathe.

OUR HALLOWED HALL

Help Yourself. Communing with Spirit during your quiet time confirms your oneness with Most High. Spirit gives spiritual support as you are moving into the mind of God.

Arrange a private space where you will not be disturbed. Make it personal and comfortable so that you are peaceful. If you sit, or if you prefer to lie down, you won't feel any discomfort. Now as you begin to relax, do not get upset if you're experiencing nervousness, hearing creaking outside or any other sounds in the world. This is a natural occurrence especially when the body is not accustomed to being in stillness and silence for any length of time. As you continue with your practice, you will begin moving into a state of personal quietude.

Remember, your environment best suits you when you take time to make it your loving space. You may enjoy having green plants, soft music playing or whatever you choose to enhance your loving time. Spirit is requiring that you do all that is good for your outer environment. It is a definite expression of who you are inside.

Once you have established order in your communing space you are ready to look upon the whole of your Being. You are ready to see your life, the fleshform of the female in which the aliveness of God is loving. Sister, don't hesitate to commend yourself. *You are the one now.* Spirit is breathing itself as you.

Look at yourself. Don't be afraid to touch every place God lives. Places you may not have wanted to see, view them. Know you are a child of God, a Daughter of the Most High, a fleshform created to house God's living Spirit.

Beloved Daughter, as you are seeing who God is as you, *see commitment*. See the word spelled out, encompassing and holding you securely. In this inner sanctuary you are already validated, already acknowledged as one created to be within this universe. You are being taught that as you release hurts, harmful activities, and painful memories, and replace them with joyfilling enthusiasm for your aliveness, you are already practicing **loving works**. Yes, dear Sister, you are truly a work of a great artist.

Therefore, **never again** will you demean yourself by adopting any forms of abusiveness. Sisters cannot support nor survive destructive behavior anytime, for any reason, as long as you are alive.

Spirit is communicating with you about being a Temple of God. You are **Our** Hallowed Hall. You are being birthed anew and this is your practice in which Divine veneration becomes you.

As you become relaxed and comforting to you, Sister, you begin cherishing the body. You know your skin is lovely, a beautiful organ covering one who realizes she is blessed. Grace becomes you.

Oh, Sister, make your time with Spirit a daily practice for grace. See what your God is giving you. There is a sweetness within, coming through and it's sweeter than honey. The first taste of this sweetness starts when you truly sense the meaning of love and order in your life. Knowing how good your life is makes it difficult to settle for anything disorderly.

Committing to **loving spiritual living** is your fourth step. **Dedication** is your key. Your command word: **Discipline**.

ESTABLISHING ORDER IN YOUR LIFE

Order begins with honesty. Being honest with yourself allows you the right to step beyond the flesh, noting everything you are prepared to get rid of to maintain peacefulness in your life's surroundings.

Spirit speaks to you about irresponsible relationships, ones in which you have invested your time yet haven't received the valuable goods which usually come from personal sharing: positive words of encouragement, emotional or creative support, networking information and innovative and beneficial ideas.

Time out, Sister. How are you measuring appreciation? Does it come, for example, only when your employer's executive assistant asks you to do a "special" favor for her for which she later receives the benefits? Are you a regular for giving away your blessings? Are you always the one not giving herself enough credit? Matter of fact, are you the one who down plays her valuable contributions? What about your valued time, your worth in terms of dollars? Are you the one who always says, "oh, it's alright, no problem," when you know how time consuming some favors can be?

You're the one who can be counted on, yet you're always feeling left out, forgotten, or discounted when exciting things are happening. Perhaps this sounds like a commercial but it is time you give yourself a break today. Starting now. Put your life in order, making lists (in case it's more than one), checking them twice and being honest about who is nasty and who is nice.

Beloved, check yourself. Your daily practice assists you in keeping order in your life by revealing what must be released and thrown out. By casting out mess you can see clearly. You know how to arrange your time, you know who you enjoy being with and you know who is rational and who is bordering on the edge of insanity. Order requires consistency. You cannot maintain your life in a haphazard manner, jumping back to the old ways for whatever reason: someone's feelings have been hurt, another person is pouting when you are no longer taking care of their duties or responsibilities, or you miss being a people pleaser.

Well, what does order contribute to your loving works? When there is order in your life, Beloved, you will recognize any form of clutter, bedlam, mayhem and disorder. Sister, you will recognize things and humans who are intrusive and disturbing to your peace and serenity. You can see who and what is out of order. You are given spiritual consciousness to protect your life from invaders. You learn to trust what you are sensing. This trusting comes from within.

It matters not what some humans consider convenient for them, and there are many humans who are very good at knowing what is perfect for someone else's time. Is there anyone who you can name today that you have allowed opportunities to create distraction and disorder in your life? Well, you know what you've got to do, Sister. What are you going to do to rid your life of the inconvenience? Here is a hint: There is no greater inconvenience than disobeying Divine Spirit!

> *I will stop focusing on everyone else first and look within.*
> *I will not seek validation from others.*
> *My worthiness comes from loving Spirit,*
> *presence and source of my aliveness.*

Help Yourself. What will you give in service to yourself today, dear Sister? Will you be effective in dishing out self approval? Is loving you important or are you giving more thought to others?

Helping yourself means you affirm loving, allowing others to share their love and happiness with you which in turn becomes assets to your life. Proclaim your spiritual rights and make your life a grateful experience. When there is order in your life, accomplishing for your personal gain comes easily. You can see clearly. You know who you are. You can see where you are going because you know where you do not have to be. You know how irrational some things have been simply because you were denying your life. Stop seeking awards from others especially when you are the one who has been keeping things in order for them.

Aha, Sister, your greatest award, your sweetest victory and your most magnificent reward comes when you look into your loving eyes and a trusting soul is smiling at you. Read your affirmation patiently and with enthusiasm. You are not being rushed, pushed, or demanded to move faster than you choose. You are within Divine order now. Are you ready, Child? Breathe easily. Relaxing. Now...

> *Congratulations, Sister.*
> *Girl, you done good.*
> *Your work is great.*
> *Your time is valuable.*
> *And I (state your name here)*
> *Reward you with love today.*

REJOICE WITH YOU!

This is the order of your day. **Rejoice with you!** This is your time for appreciation, adoration and applause. Lets hear it. *Applaud for you, Beloved.* Lets hear that joy coming forth. Lets see God's aliveness expressing itself as you. *Applaud for you, Beloved.* Oh, what a treasure you are, what a blessing for one who will always acknowledge her presence as the image of God: A First World Wombman maintaining order in her life.

ALWAYS REMEMBER WHO YOU ARE

It's time, Sisters. Time to make the greatest step you've ever given thought to complete. It is time to make your leap of faith and begin, immediately, seeing the beauty of God right where you are. When any one of us does not appreciate, with love, all that we are given, we become destroyers of our spiritual lineage. You cannot continue breathing, being ashamed and afraid to acknowledge your worthiness. While we are creating our own mean spirited ways for self disapproval, remember there are others armed, bombarding us **daily** with negativity, determined to assist us in believing the worst about ourselves.

60
▼▼▼

What has happened that Sisters would continually give credence to any humans who would have you believe you are lesser, minorities, **no** things? For example: Sisters are becoming lucrative fodder for television talk shows. It seems there is no respect and fifteen minutes or less of fame has given some Sisters reason to air everything from personal sexual fantasies to all but strangling another Sister or whatever action will bring about her visual disgrace.

Now what does this say about loving? Have you watched any Sister screaming, cussing and hurling vindictively abusive words at her *enemy* as well as the audience? Do you cringe or are you ranting and raving along with her? Do you question why we would desire to condemn each other and denigrate ourselves before the world? Are we so hungry for attention? Do we expect the world will offer solutions to our problems when we are acting worse than dogs in throes of heat? Throw the Sister a bone. This is all she wants.

Are we that desperate? Are Sisters suffering from so many misconceptions of unworthiness until they would destroy any semblance of self–worth and respectability?

Remember who you are! **You are First World ascendant.** Don't get pulled into the humdrum of ignorance. You do not have to buy into other Sister's messiness. You don't have to purchase the ugliness some Sisters are selling. And stop supporting other Sisters who are being sold.

Remember who you are! **Sisters have come to far to be disgraceful in God's presence.**

> I am First World Ascendant.
> My God's presence in fleshform, female human.
> Daughter of Divine Spirit.
> I remember who I am.

I am coming this day with grace.
There is everything sacred about me.
I am _____
(Sign your name)

COMMIT TO THE GOOD LIFE

Give time to you so that the quality of your life gets better day by day. Keep your immediate surroundings, your environment, peaceful—where you have peace it is easier to reason and irrational actions cannot survive. Do not allow anything or anyone to bring confusion, commotion, or any stifling attitudes.

The sooner you release yourself, God's Aliveness, from intrusive individuals who bring negativity, the quicker you will have the time you previously thought was not available. Cleaning mess out gives plenty of space for you to fill with good self loving. There comes a sense of personal priority when you choose to live and love with peace. There is more time given to keeping peace and calmness wherever you be. It's you. It becomes you and it breathes you. Whatever Sister chooses to do to keep joy within her home, self preservation is first. The one important rule to remember is: **Your home is a spiritual domain. Your home is you.**

No human at any time is allowed to disturb your domain. The quality of your life is your personal responsibility, your own creation. You are in ownership of how you choose to spend your time. Love and peace are precious. They are staples, as necessary as food and water. Spirit requires concentration on the Goddess self so that peace comes naturally and loving self becomes a permanent acknowledgement.

Begin to see the physical as more than body. It is **You = Your Own Universe.** You are priority. Spirit was breathing itself as your life prior to your birth. You are birthed from the mind of God and limitless in your spiritual expressing. Therefore, it becomes your principal duty to respond to the care and preservation of God's life. **You = Your Own Universe**.

In other words, Sister, treat your life to the best. Committing to **creating good for you** is your fifth step. **Victory** is your key! Your command word: **Viable**.

Emotional Captivity

This is my time to be loving Me.
I am free to love Me.
I am freely loved by God.

The only truth is your soul's truth. Whether this truth presents adverse reactions or stimulates sensations of joy, your soul cannot lie. Your soul is evidence of an illustrious power possessing life as you. You are your life; there is no way to get around this fact. No matter how human's try they cannot get away from their soul's truth.

Put a face on your truth and dwell within silence for an instant—silence can be more powerful than loud words and emotional outbursts. From this moment on, you will cast out evil before it can get a hold in your life. You will witness God's power in action. As your life is an ongoing process, let us put what we are knowing into its most powerful purpose.

It is time to **Help Yourself** by closing the door to thoughts of woe and constraint. You do not have to allow contrary provocations to disturb your peace. Rebuke antagonizing messiness. Stop! Breathe, Beloved.

GOD IS MY STRENGTH *and all things are possible.*

Within me are unlimited possibilities ready to come forth.
In God my perfection is determined; and in
God's timing perfection is endless.
All things come to pass according to my willingness to receive,
my willingness to accept and my dedication to achieving all that
is good and perfect in God's sight for my personal well being.
GOD IS MY STRENGTH

TIME TO BE REMARKABLE, SISTER

Are you a Sister who is chosen yet reluctant to acclaim your self? Are you hesitant with self appreciation? How many times have you willfully reverted into thoughts about those sorrowful days of yesteryear, those times when tears were regular companions, friends were few and for whatever reasons you did not believe your life was important within the universe?

Ummmm, hummmmm. Beloved, Spirit is speaking to you about being held captive in wasteful thinking, lackluster activities and atrocious relationships. Spirit is speaking to you about being bound, enslaved and mired in endless hassles and seeing no way out.

Well, Sister it is possible to have your chaos and beat it too. With God and Loving Spirit Divine you can make it through. You've got to, got to, got to see God's good about you. Are you ready, Beloved?

First, you will rid yourself of that enslaved mentality, limiting thinking, thoughtless ideas and disbelief about your personal strengths. Let us not get too comfortable putting your loving heritage on hold. Straighten yourself, Sister, and look beyond the past. Can you see where you have emerged from? Are you willing to see a female human wearing a skin tone so lovely until the universe calls out your name?

Spirit speaks about you this morning, Sister. Spirit is calling out to you so that you will understand what it is to be memorable. Look at you. Look at your physical body. Look at your whole being. Look beyond any faults, any disfigurement, or anything you formerly perceived to be ugly. Look and see who God is freeing you to be. Who is this face in front of you? Whose eyes are looking inside? What manner of life are you living, Sister? Why are you still crying?

Oh, Beloved, come into God's world. Come within the soul's place and hear, with tenderness, new thoughts about your aliveness. See one deserving and knowing she is. Spirit is speaking about you *to* you. She is surrounding you with a listening quality, telling you how important you are.

You must recollect your positive dreams. Recall your impressiveness, your ability to believe your presence is necessary for the world's to come. Yes, first be cleansed of any things creating enslavement. It's your time to be remarkable, Sister.

> *My life is my meditation.*
> *My breath is my prayer.*
> *I look outward from within.*
> *And I see my Presence in God.*
> *I know...*
> *I am divine Presence of God.*

ABUSE IS NOT LOVE

What is your name, Daughter? What are you called? Have you suffered any degradation or slights from any human who would tear your life asunder simply because they believe you are agreeing to abide in negativity? Have you given any man or woman cause to thrust their brutal anger or venomous hostilities toward you simply because they believe you are available? Have you allowed any one to disturb your peace or invade your sanctity with vile words and heart breaking language simply because you have refused to speak up about your God life?

What about individuals who use any reason to hit, knock, stomp, kick, slap, curse, spit, or use any other actions you know are terrifying? Are you receiving that choking, unkind loving? You don't have anything like this going on in your life, do you, Sister?

These are not admirable traits. Many Sisters are unwilling to be complacent punching bags. They are not open for experimentation to see how long they can endure pain and suffering. There is not **one** thing honorable or heroic about abuse. Valiant victimization is not a cause for reverence.

Abuse is not love.

TAKE A STAND FOR LIFE.

Alright now. Come on with it. Tell these children about God loving. Tell them the time is here when all Daughters of First World Diaspora are coming to build new worlds beginning with spiritually secured relationships.

Spirit Holy is commanding Sisters to depart from illusions about love and take a stand for life. You are not dark deep holes into which loveless seeds are thrown. You are God's life. When you uphold your life you'll know what love is. For example: Visualize your innumerable ancestresses holding up blood-stained standards, victoriously rebuking any activities thought to be life enslaving. See these Wombman struggling yet loving. They were being signs of your presence today. Are they promoting ways of weakness or are they fearless in their strides? Are you as passionate about your future?

Do you see your Mothers there, your Grand Grandmothers? These are your great life bearers. Weren't you there, Sister?

Are not you alive in Spirit's infinite substance? These life givers bled for your life! These life givers tilled the earth for you.

Spirit told them you would be born. It was during those difficult times a loving bond was already created. They fought for your right to live and to love, Daughter. Your divine breath was alive, formed in the mind of God. And although you had yet to be conceived, Beloved, God was transmitting your coming radiance. This light is your life. And this light is powerfilling.

MotherSisters believed for you! With the power of God within them and the breath of Divine Spirit guiding them, their love has brought you into being. Are you as believing today as they were for you yesterday?

Spirit is speaking about securing your stronghold for life. And here you are. Remember who you are, Black Wombman. Remember who you are. These mothers shed blood. They came through hidden doorways so that you would live without fear. Remember your relationship with God and Holy Spirit. This union supreme is your measuring rod. A lasting love, strong and mightfilled. Remember who you are, Black Wombman. **Remember who you are!**

> *I am thankful for Holy Spirit comforting me*
> *during times of stress, complaints and worry.*
> *She is translating her work as I am.*
> *I know I am a loving Child of God.*
> *I truly know I am.*
> *And I don't mind saying so...*

DUMP FOR JOY!

This is the page where Sister gets rid of any feelings, thoughts, persons, or anything that makes you feel constriction or personal afflictions. Dump any negative or hostile feelings toward any human and subconscious constipation stuff you may not be aware of.

Your **Dump for Joy** page is for total and complete relief. It is also a great way of making amends, forgiving self and others. *Atonement.*

The way you **Help Yourself** is by bagging and trashing. Gather your disillusions and any confusion, negative qualities and limited thinking and burn all the mess.

DUMP FOR JOY!

I am dumping this mess to free me. Whatever it is, my lack or fear, I no longer accept being bound with or in it. I have no doubts surrounding my life. I deserve to be free and I release, affirming NO *thing is binding me. I am dumping for joy:*

_____

_____

_____

_____

_____

_____

_____

_____

_____

* *For additional dumping, use blank pages at the back of the book.*

Signature: _____

My freedom date is: _____ 19___

I have dumped for joy!!!!!

I am **FREE. FREE. FREE. FREE. FREE.**

Thank God, I am free.

This is my time to be loving me.
I am free to love me (state your name).
I am freely loved by my God.

YOUR VICTORIOUS DECLARATION.

Help Yourself, Beloved. Look into a mirror. If the declaration applies to you, repeat it twenty–five times and see a healed Wombman.

Abuse is not love.
Abuse is out of my life.
Abuse is not love.
Abuse is not in my life.

After you have spoken your words, be sure you have an understanding about them. Why do these words affect you? Is there anyone you know struggling within an abusive situation? What can you do to assist this individual? Are children involved? Are you acquainted with a Sister who is grieving because she believes, for whatever reason, that she is deserving of mistreatment? Could there be an underlying problem requiring therapy, psychological, medical or spiritual help?

If you are answering "Yes," then it is time to make a change. If it is you, Beloved, it is time to get help.

72
▼▼▼

You do not want to see a loved one––SisterMother DaughterNeiceCousinAuntieGirlFriendCo–worker––brutalized. **Abuse is not love.**

Spirit is speaking about the times when you have not wanted to be bothered and did not want to involve yourself in others' traumas. When one is hurt by any abusive actions, all who love and care are in pain. They may not have been physically, mentally or spiritually touched, but within they are feeling the brute force of the abuse. Beloved, should you hesitate to get involved for any reason, then send a loving card or a handwritten note assuring your Sister there are many ways in which help comes. You must reach out and share your life saving information.

Can you remember a time when you attempted to be helpful and this was the very moment your good intentions were taken for granted, misconstrued as nosiness, bothersome and none of your business? Whether we choose to believe or not, Beloved, there are some humans who love danger, destruction and unlawful living. You can relate to our meaning here: Your good intentions just were not wanted.

Empathy can get you down. Yes, it can wear you out, whip you to a frazzle just as the ones whom you are hoping to rescue are being abused. What do you do when you know a loved one is being hurt? Do you back off, run away, or do you make their battle yours?

How many times have you resisted getting involved yet have been willing and determined to race into quarrels created because of someone else's choices? How does it feel when you are putting on armor and shield to fight a battle which is not yours?

For example: Sister Savior is running to the rescue. Beloved has become the ultimate paramedic regarding human traumas. You are hearing a resounding, "**No!**", an objective, "**Let it Be!**", yet you feel you have got to do something. You do not want to see anyone hurting. These are times which try women's souls.

You are remembering who you are. There are lives to be saved. You are the only trooper. You have come a long way now and you are trying to reach an irrational, confused person. An individual dedicated to creating chaos. You are hearing a resounding, "**Let it Be!**" Despite desperation you have thought about that day when it could have been you. Maybe yesterday it was you. Today it need not be your life.

Spirit is practical; Spirit is not emotional. What does this mean? Spirit is speaking to you about knowing when to leave situations alone in order to secure your personal wellness. While others are continuing to fight for their right to self destruct and **you have done all you can do**, Holy Spirit is advising you to be still and removed from your emotions. Spirit is speaking to you about outside circumstances that can be personally eroding to your life. Destruction is going on, havoc is being reaped. And you have got to live.

You are being requested to seek calmness. **Be still and listen.** In stillness you move into your quiet space of familiarity, sensing God's securing power, allowing you the privilege of knowing everything is exactly as it should be for you. Do not get despondent about being unable to help someone who seems lost and forlorn.

The practicality of Divine Spirit does not require the surrendering of your spiritual nature. When you listen to Spirit you will always be lead righteously. As you are listening, you are being reminded of who you are. You are not called to be immersed in pain resulting from humans who are disobedient and willing to believe they must suffer to receive love. Abuse is not love.

God helps in times of very present danger. Therefore, when you are moved to get involved and you know the voice of Spirit is leading, you can be assured you are on the righteous track. Sister's presence will be welcomed. Your goodness will be acknowledged and appreciated. And your light will shine for others to see God's loving works through you.

Spirit, which keeps you, commands **no guiltiness** when

you have given your very best. Beloved, you know your best is God's good. Remember who you are!

Committing to **acknowledging my life daily** is my sixth step. **Believing in you** is your key! Your command word: **Trust.**

Power of Black Wombman

It is time for me to get to stepping.
I am securing myself in this bold new age.

Dearest Sister, Spirit is speaking about Declaring your Place Of Veneration. **POV** involves everything good, pure and righteous about you. Your positive Point Of View about your life, your Points Of Virtue and your Precious Omnipotent Vagina. (To venerate = to hold in exalted honor without fear)

Before we begin with your **POV,** there is one question which must be answered. Did you, at any time during your living, select a disparaging lifestyle or entertain a self abasing episode? If so, Beloved, this is your spiritual exoneration. You are not required nor commanded to entertain humiliation forever.

God is calling for Virtuous Sisters. Cleansed. Lucid. Victorious. Regardless of your wants and desires, regardless of any wanton or past fallen ways, despite situations of (seemingly) prevailing sadness, regardless of your belief that you are alone, regardless of children born out of wedlock, regardless of horrific names you have been called, regardless of hunger and thirsting for attention...*are you tiring, Sister?*...regardless of how you trusted untrustworthy humans or regardless of how physical handicaps or symptoms of illness and ailments may be misunderstood, regardless of how you have been disappointed or rejected, regardless of crumbling and disorderly world systems, regardless of death and dying, Beloved....What are you doing about loving your life?

No human can put a label or tag on you without your acceptance. Beloved, it does not matter what anyone has said about your life. Regardless of how you may have attempted to fit into some typical mode of powerlessness, believe God knows you personally. God knew what you could achieve before you were conceived.

No human can replace God's soul. Spirit is embracing you at this very moment. To make your entrance into enlightenment, You should not deny this or you will be denying a most wonderfilling relationship. You are Our heart, the very existence of God in presence of female human, Beloved. First Creation. First Sign. First Wombman. First Blood. First Ancestress. First Ascendant. First, Black Womb-man, know yourself.

Beloved, any violation you may have committed against yourself or any person whom you believe or know to have vilified or violated you, release them. Choose not to go against Spirit's inner guidance and you will see personal transgressions eradicated. Free your mind.

Black Wombman, do not praise inferiority. Protect yourself by willingly releasing any weaknesses you may think you have.

Most High breathed Godliness, Grace and Goodwill into your lips. You are entitled to these life loving qualities. They are yours, intricately woven into your soul.

Your **P**oints **O**f **V**irtue command you to live in higher consciousness.

79
▼▼▼

Your **P**oints **O**f **V**irtue commands that you concentrate on your positive attributes.

Beloved, never deny your blessings. You should all ways cherish your **POV**.

BLACK WOMBMAN'S POINT OF VIEW

Beloved is not designated to initiate
pride for being classified as minority.

What is Spirit speaking about when referring to the Black Wombman's **P**oint **O**f **V**iew? Definitely not glorifying and praising a lesser than consciousness. Throughout Sister's life Black has **never** been used to denote purity, strength, splendor, nor brilliance. Minority conscious individuals need to understand the word "black" carries stigma of evil, life long suffering, sadness, perversion and death. Do you know any Sisters' who are partying hearty in celebration of being a minority? Sister must know this miscategorization is not a prerequisite for celebrating her existence. Would God have created First World Wombman blemished, without backbone, and then banish her into obscurity? What is this about?

If you choose to effectively raise your position in life, you must first honor your life. Negative thinking is destructive; positive thoughts are constructive. Your Divine power authorizes you to be fearless and daring when you define your life. Your **P**oint **O**f **V**iew, to which you are entitled, can imprison or empower you.

From now on the former definition of *Blackness* is no longer applicable to God's First World Wombman's aliveness. Spirit commands Sister to wear her Blackness with impeccable dignity. Spirit has given Sister fortitude and tenacious ability to establish her **Point Of View** by creating new meaning in her world. Spirit is speaking to Sister about elevating Blackness to its supreme place. This is not difficult to do because the Blackness is about your faith and power of love. Will you make these things your life's **Point Of View**?

Divine Spirit requires you to extend yourself beyond the outer world. We want you to move through the powerful darkness knowing God, giver of your living breath, brought you from Divine inception into this moment to know, Beloved, Black is beautiful!

> *Spirit commands Sister to wear her*
> *Blackness with impeccable dignity.*

To **Help Yourself**, clear your mind by moving into quiet time. Become centered so that you can concentrate in silence. Within your quiet space We ask that you review any things you consider personal *losses*—acquaintances, jobs, relationships, any dismal descriptions, whatever—and begin to visualize your spiritual gains.

Sister, listen to Spirit speaking within your heart and soul. Relax and become comfortable with what you are hearing. This is your mind's time. It is important that you trust what you are being given. Divine Spirit is about stimulating an entirely different truth within you, a positive, powerful and faithfilling **Point Of View**.

81
▼▼▼

GOOD INTENTIONS REQUIRE
GREATER INCENTIVES.

The way in which your **Point Of View** will manifest is through faith and faith depends on your **Point Of View**. Perhaps faith may not be a conscious focus for you on a daily basis. Faith may not be a physical item that you see or on which you can place your hands, however, faith will become evident as soon as you surrender your physical and mental body to God.

Faith's tangible presence is evident because you are alive. If you are alive then your faith can be immediately activated. Are you breathing, Sister?

Your dreams, hopes and desires must be of a spiritual nature. Clear thoughts originate from Divine Spirit, that mind centering place of God. A spiritual **P**oint **O**f **V**iew commands that you be alert. This way you will always come out ahead.

Faith requires personal works along with trusting and believing. Without works, actions and deeds, faith is null and void. No thing happens, no thing manifests unless you are involved spiritually, mentally and physically. These three in one actions are inseparable and guaranteed to manifest fine results, satisfactory and fulfilling to Sister's desires. Good intentions require greater incentives. Are you lucid, Beloved?

As you continue trusting it becomes obvious the ease in which you and Spirit work together. God, Spirit and you are inseparable. All that is righteously created for your life will manifest for your good, grace and prosperity. You will receive whatever things are beneficial for fulfillment of your life purpose.

82 ▼▼▼ Beloved, **You are strong, victorious and unstoppable**. If you were not would so many be willing to have you believe the worst of whatever your existence is purported to be? It's time, Sister, for you to see yourself accepting God's good as your divine due. Look at your life and claim your power.

Spirit's **P**oint **O**f **V**iew, to which you are entitled, is a blessing to your existence because it transcends all physical or mental limitations established by you. Spirit is embracing your life at this very moment, making you stronger. Therefore, when you review your life see faith, graciousness and a victorious Black Wombman. Compose yourself and change your **P**oint **O**f **V**iew.

> *I am a virtuous Wombman.*
> *I love myself.*
> *I am spiritually blessed.*
> *Everything works in my favor.*
> *Spirit's Point Of View is surrounding me.*
> *Spirit's vision is my POV.*

FIRST SIGN

Spirit speaks: God's work may seem to you, Beloved, to be profound yet it is a regular happening. To many it is eventful and miraculous. However, when you are centered within you will know these occurrences are *nature all*, a daily manifesting for those who trust God. Wonderfilling and awe inspiring activities are ever and all ways available to those having faith. When you are searching for signs and wonders, Sister, you need look no further than breathing. It is the only sign you need to see that you, yes, even you, are a wonder, a miracle of life.

When looking for signs of assurance you may never be granted the opportunities to see what you're expecting because your personal expectation may not be the first thing required for you to have a spiritual life. Believing is key to your life experiences. When you believe in Divine Spirit you are given inner sight. You will see. Though many choose not to acknowledge what is valuably revealed and traipse on into turmoil, they are still knowledgeable about truth. The most prevalent sign is trusting what you are given from Spirit. You become **focus**.

You are not taking anything for granted when you trust;

your gifts, goods and talents, and those abilities blessed. For example, your determination to succeed where many are breathing expectations of failure and words of hopelessness: "I told you it wouldn't work," "You're never going to get it," or "You'd better pray for a sign." Beloved, *you are first sign.* Stop looking for others to be wonderfilling for you. Choose to accept your spiritual advantages; live in consciousness of competence. You are first sign.

When seeking personal advantages have mercy on self. God's Will reveals Sister. Believe. You are first sign. Believe. You are soul representative of who you are, who you hope to be, how you think you must be. You. Sister, it's you.

Therefore, when seeking signs, searching, sweating, panting, frothing and foaming at the mouth, crying, whining, tearing hair on or off, screaming, dependent on panicking, know that through it all, Sister is **focus**. Through it all keep hoping, having faith and trusting, have mercy on self and choose to accept spiritual progress. *You are first sign.*

> *I am first sign. This wisdom moves me to attain my goal.*
> *I am first sign. This wisdom moves*
> *me to have patience with myself.*
> *I accept my spiritual progress.*
> *I am first sign.*

84
▼▼▼

My name is:_____

FAITH ACCOMPLISHMENTS

Beloved, now is your time for creating and achieving. When you feel rested and in a state of ease follow through by filling in Your Faith Accomplishment sheet. You do not have to complete your page in a single swoop. Take your time; do not rush. Just be sure you are in a peaceful faith filled state of mind when you fill in your lines.

1. _____
2. _____
3. _____
4. _____
5. _____
6. _____
7. _____
8. _____
9. _____
10. _____
11. _____
12. _____
13. _____
14. _____
15. _____
16. _____
17. _____
18. _____
19. _____
20. _____
21. _____

With God all things are possible. I Believe this.
I know this to be my truth. I have faith.
I am letting Spirit have its way.
Everyday I am thankful, filled and
overflowing with God's divine grace.
I deserve my good. And I readily receive it.
I am a FaithfilledPowerworkingVictoriouslyVirtuous
NewlifeDefiningWombman of the Blackness.

RESPECT YOUR BLACK SELF

Respect God's life, Daughter. Respect Divine Spirit as the only life you are today. Respect your Black self. **B**rilliant **L**oving**A**ttractive**C**apable**K**een. *I respect my Black self!*

Sister is holding a preeminent position within new world. Be glad. Be elated. Be happy. Be joy filled. Be grateful. Be appreciative. Be awareness. Be knowledgeable. Be wisdom. Be loving. Be God's goodness. *I respect my Black self!*

Brilliant**L**oving**A**ttractive**C**apable**K**een. First World Ascendant**S**ign**W**ombman**C**reator**D**aughter**S**ister**G**irl**C**hild. Wake up, **First Sign**. Wake from that drowsy, slow to move, fearful of taking a stand to gather power with, for and among your Sisters. Are you awake now? Breathe, Sister. Breathe. Are you breathing, Sister? Breathe, please. And believe Holy Spirit is transforming you **now**. The days of self depreciation, trading insults and denying Sister life and love is **OVER**: **O**ut**V**anquished**E**rased**R**efused. *I respect my Black self!*

It is time for me to get to stepping.
I am securing myself in this bold new age.
Faith, believing, trusting and knowing
makes all good things possible for:

Signature_____

Committing to my **positive new way of thinking**, my **positive new way of behaving** and my **positive new way of acknowledging my Godlife** is my seventh step. **Trusting my inner voice** is my key. My command word: **Awake**.

Ordained Relationships

Beloved, speak these words aloud:

> *God's work is done.*
> *God's work is done.*
> *God's work is done.*
> *I don't have to be concerned about a thing*
> *nor do I have a worry in life.*
> *I will never devalue my life.*
> *I will never allow any human to devalue my life.*
> *I love myself unconditionally.*
> *Thank God.*

By speaking your words, Sister, you are establishing your verbal agreement between you, God and Holy Spirit. You cannot take your words back; you cannot renege on your contract. Should you attempt to do so you will find yourself suffering, worrying and doubtful about the smallest things. Do not wear yourself into bouts of aggravation and pain, depression and heartaches. You are not born to suffering all your days, crying and feeling body broken in midnight hours. No, Beloved, this is not God's will nor the way of loving Spirit for your life.

I am in my righteous relationship.
I am a loving definition of Divine Spirit.
God loves me as Herself, myself and His self.
I Be. I see.
I know me and I breathe loving Sister unconditionally.

Signature:_____

Date:_____

Time:_____am_____pm

LIVING A SPIRITUAL LIFE

Treasures of heaven are right where I am.
I rejoice, living my life freely and responsibly.
Responsibility requires no doubt within,
about or surrounding me.

You are created in the image of your Creator. In this like-ness of God, you are given to know that eternal life has its beginning within your fleshform. And as long as Spirit lives, having Her being as you, Daughter, you have a right to be rev-erent of your aliveness.

You are breathing rules of right living and these internal laws are written within your soul. Beloved can sense the differ-ence between righteous and unrightful living. Being a Daughter of First World, you are given a charge to **Never Forget**: *My life is God's life.*

The spiritual transformation of your life begins immediate-ly when you change the ways in which you create your thoughts. You were created in an uplifted movement, raised from the darkest of earth's beauty. Beloved's beauty is yet evi-dent. You are God's life. Accept who you are. To know yourself and to know what you desire most in the world, while at the same time you are fearful and suspect of your spiritual power, is cause for concern. This is why it is your obligation to return to the source of your aliveness. Do not be afraid to look within your heart and soul to see any impossibilities eradicated.

You are being set right, Beloved. Spirit is putting your life in loving order because it is time you recognize yourself. You are Spirit's radiance. You don't have to worry nor become stressed about whether you can live up to your sacred designation. If you could not attain your divine position, Beloved, you would not be breathing at this moment. Breathe, Sister. Breathe.

WITH GOD ALL THINGS ARE POSSIBLE.

Spirit gives good love.

Without any previous or past insecurities intervening you are being requested *not* to ask any human for love and blessings. You are being requested to establish a loving vow between you, God and Spirit Holy. Immediately, Sister. Breathe.

From birth God receives your requests. When you are praying for a loving relationship, listing all the prerequisites, the don't wants and must haves, all you have to do is ask for God's ordained relationship. When you are trusting and having faith, believe! And as you are securely breathing in your faith and knowing, Beloved, believe! You will see marvelous blessings *unfolding* you.

Are you available to recieve your God's good? Are you holding confidently to your trust, knowing no thing at any time, for any reason can move you from your believing? When you're immersed in this consciousness, you become a loving attraction. Your loving relationship begins with and within you. You will find yourself unable to settle for anything less.

Every cell in Beloved's body breathes: *I believe. I am living my ordained relationship.* Breathe, Sister. Breathe.

Now, again, repeat your words: *Every cell in my body breathes I believe. I am loving my ordained relationship.*

Sister, Spirit speaks on a few points which have to do with recognition and respect of your magnetic connection. It's important to understand how powerful this position is. You are determined, reaffirming daily, your *sticktoitiveness* regarding your ordained relationship. You're ready for loving now that you, God and Spirit have got it going on. You see your life changing, knowing that as your positive plans are manifesting you are exuding sweet fragrances of femininity, acknowledging adoring glances and inquiries while still trying to maintain the subtleties of spiritual living.

Spirit wants you to know about temptation which can be more than you choose to bear, especially when it is tapping your invisible vulnerable places. Temptation can be an incredible foe when you are determined to stick to your loving agreements. Your faith gets tried and tested. You want to be held and touched. Sister feels she is ready for love, ready for love, just ready. The external world forces are beating paths to your door and you feel like retreating into any space of security. Oh, Sister, stuff is popping out everywhere. You want to be making love when you know no lover is around.

You're praying, meditating and flesh is craving, demanding to be satisfied. Desire is sneaking through you when you're asleep and you can hear your brain repeating your affirmation: *I do believe I have my ordained relationship.* It is more than a notion, isn't it? Emotions are demanding to be attended to; what good is a signed agreement when Beloved's body is screaming to be touched, held and kissed? What good is an agreement when

Sister feels like sneaking around and spending time with some-body's significant other who is sneaking around? Be strong, Daughter. Breathe: *I do believe I have my ordained relationship*. Let Spirit help during these troubling times, Sister. Stick to your contract. This is why you sign your agreements.

Uh Huh. It's rough sometimes. Nobody said it was going to be easy, Beloved. You've got to work with you. And you've got the will within. Now is your time to see spiritual work being done. Within you the good work is complete. These are the interim times when you are trying to keep the faith, trying to keep hopeful, trying to hold on to God's unchanging hand....Trying and you're feeling it's futile, these weak stabs at keeping your life together. Remember today, last night, the other month? It seems as if every step you're making is feeble and you're tired. Just one moment, Sister. Are you wanting val-idation so deeply that you'd rather give up than keep on believ-ing? If your answer is truthful and you've responded, "Yes!", you're doing excellent work. You're acknowledging Womb-man's humaness.

You are not hiding, putting on airs like you've got it togeth-er when you're anxious, distraught, and still tired. Too difficult. Too weakening. Too rough. Everything feels like it's falling apart. Believing? Ordained relationship? How can I keep on believing? Why should I continue to believe?

Why should Sister not believe? You and God are partners. Truth friends. Trusting companions. Spirit Divine is your coun-selor, comforter and loving consoler.

Spirit is requesting you to listen to your heart, Sister. Your ordained relationship comes by way of faith which calls forth your personal desire to trust. A Sister who believes must continue doing so because all she has is her ability to believe. No man or Wombman can remove this awareness. Humans can do all they will to deter your believing, doing all to contribute negatives so that you will cease trusting, but you are the only one who can give up. Hold on, Beloved! You may release believing, yet believing will never let you go. As long as **you** believe you can change things: situations, circumstances, environment, surroundings, friends, business associates, family, lovers. Everything incorporates relationships. You are in control of your believing. You are birthed with this ability. It is innate, Beloved. It **IS!**

Spirit requests that you not give up. Be hopeful. Talk good talk to you. Believe you are love, Sister. Wear your loving truth knowing you are influenced by Spirit. She is guiding you. Are you secured within this sweetness? Isn't it refreshing feeling your wholeness and realizing no thing can make you stray from unconditionally loving your life?

When you depend on God, you are entrusting your life to Divine intervention: a lifetime guaranty within a supportive system which is unfailing. Committing to **cherishing health and physical wellbeing** is my permanent step. **Keeping God's presence alive** is my key. My command word: **Vibrant**.

> *God spoke my life into being.*
> *I am never in need of the love*
> *I am ordained to receive.*
> *My relationships are blessings:I know this*
> *for I have my loving time guaranteed.*

95
▼▼▼

Signature:_____

Oh, Dearly Beloved, Child of Most High, know in this present time God's will has to come forth for you. Believe. And

be the embodiment of all you are speaking. Are you ready, Sister? If you are, take the following to heart:

> *Holy Spirit is sooooooo good to me.*
> *Today I am fulfilled as a woman, a divine Sister.*
> *I, female human, am blessed from inception with authority*
> *and power to choose rightfully all that is good for my life.*
> *I surrender any things, all things which caused me to previously*
> *believe I had to be enslaved to lesser than thinking.*
> *My achievements come by way of God's grace.*
> *I live, breathe and have my Being within God's life.*
> *I am my Ordained Relationship.*

9

Intimacy

Sexual intimacy is the closest your
soul comes to realizing heaven on earth.

Spirit speaks of **sex** being your utmost **s**elfless **ex**pressing, those special times when you are sharing happiness through active desire for your loving partner. This phenomenal desire is only revealed when you reach beyond the self, extending your life and limbs, merging, sexpressing and surpassing flesh.

Intimacy requires truth, doesn't it, Sister? Sexual union is a most high action, a truth achievement where humans are not merely touching but are coming to meet themselves within each other, loving together as one soul. With Divine intimacy, Spirit moves her bodies perfectly.

100
▼▼▼

Sexual intimacy is the closest your soul comes to realizing heaven on earth. Your intimate movements may seem to be a serious physical struggle yet it is that sensual dance interpreted solely through the rhythms of your emotions as you become a co–creator with your partner.

Sexual communication is oftentimes without words yet the silent communication can be heard. It is this honesty of your feelings which cannot be denied. The deepness within your most intimate of moments can reveal what is real for you, Beloved.

Spirit speaks about establishing your soul's heaven on earth. Now, not some day far away. We are speaking about a state of mind in which your divine self is peaceful and rejoicing; a state in which you're continuously returning to your beginning. This returning is reminiscent of experiencing the greatest intimacy you've ever felt. A soulful climaxing journey, so rapturous you will never want to bring anything sexually displeasing into your life.

When God breathed aliveness into your bodies the coming together was holy. The conjoining of two souls is an enlivening sexpression of oneness and this harmonious uniting is the beginning of spiritual grace.

Sister, you are First Creator with original man. Within you he gained entrance into heaven and a sacred communion was begun. God knows Black Wombman is a very visible and influential entity representing the meaning of divine union. See to it that your intimate communion is with a truthful soul for this marks the beginning of sexual grace. And ecstasy.

Sister, can you recall the last time you subjected your body to the inconvenience of a passionless moment? You are not a nonthinking pleasure giver breathing to satisfy any hurried, unfulfilling sexual encounter. Beloved is being cautioned about sexually transmitted diseases and not being uneasy when it comes time to ask questions prior to intercourse. It is imperative to talk intelligently (with self) about these days rife with illness and death resulting from irresponsible behavior. Then come to healthy conclusions by establishing safe living rules for loving.

Is it important to know why **you** are given control over your sexual desires? Or is it important to be spontaneous and relieve desires which serve no purpose except to satisfy body hunger? Get in touch with your passion.

There are some Sisters holding on to self imposition as if it is a badge of glory. Intimacy requires sanity. Asking questions is lifesaving. Many who did not ask and could not wait are spending their lifetime in eternity. The heat of the moment does not supersede Sister's sexual security. That rush rush clothes strewn across the floor commercialized drama does not secure Sister's life. Spirit commands Sisters to be armed with information. Sanity becomes your courageous backer. And now you will be secure within your sexuality, ready to *sexpress* yourself to your soul's contentment.

Sister, you must not honor conformity more than you love your life, thus, reverence for the life God has given you is in order. You are given, from your spiritual birth, a command not to be complacent with God's life. Man nor woman controls your anointed body, Daughter. You have a duty to challenge conformity and complacency. **Help Yourself** by daring to rise above the norm. Get rid of self–deception. Today you must set higher standards for your life's time by cherishing, daily, your soul and her divine aliveness. The greater presence of God commands you to know **quality** in your life.

PERSONAL SEXPLORATION

What do you think about self–satisfaction, masturbation and personal *sexploration*, Sister? Are you getting to know your sensual body, loving your private time? What are you doing to rid yourself of those SOBs? We're not speaking about sobbing tears of emptiness. We're speaking about sins of blackness, those no nos and don't dos; those antiquated rules and myths about hands falling off if you touch yourself in personal places private to everyone but you.

Some SisterMotherFriends and relations remember when Wombman's body was not supposed to feel the heat in her loins. She was property of man and he was master of her **Precious Omnipotent Vagina.** How many of you recall that possessively demanding question: Whose p____y is this? Of course, Sister and man know POV to be hers. However, to keep man happy and stroke his enormous ego, what was your spontaneous response? "Mine" _____ or "Yours" _____. (You may fill in your answer, Beloved.)

Precious Omnipotent Vagina does not belong to man. No matter how he may yearn to have power and possession over it. No matter how many battles have been waged, friendships lost and speculations regarding who will gain entry, God gave control of the gates to you.

What is Sister doing with her most prized possession? Are you comfortable with your right to self pleasure? When is the last time you personally touched yourself familiarly with love? When was last time your loving partner touched you familiarly? Do you experience similar feelings when you are by yourself? Personal sexploration is an excellent way to get to know yourself intimately.

Mutual sexploration is your private choice and it should give you a sense of joyfilling love mentally, spiritually and physically. How well you perform your loving ritual depends on whether you believe and recognize your right to love and be loved. Spirit is encouraging you to enjoy wonderfilling love-making beginning with sexual awareness about your self first, Beloved. What do you think about this?

Today I will set higher standards for my life.
I will cherish my soul and her divine aliveness.
I will not allow my sacred life to be depreciated!

PRECIOUS OMNIPOTENT VAGINA

It's time for Wombman to honor her Precious Omnipotent Vagina. Her divine entrance is the hallowed place from which human life is birthed into the physical world.

Wombman's Precious Omnipotent Vagina holds the key which allows man to witness the beginning of life. The throne of human life is centered within Wombman's sacred entrance. And she must be protected and guarded because this is the doorway through which mankind desires to make his presence known.

Man has designed and built elaborate cathedrals, towering suspension bridges, massive nuclear power plants, and has put satellites in space: **No human can design Wombman's vagina**.

God has bestowed upon Wombman this very special place, a loving center of mysterious secrets which brings forth sustenance of life. Wombman's blood, the precious nectar of eternal life, is evidence of her might and power.

Man comes to enter Precious Omnipotent Vagina. He seeks to find himself within Wombman's body. In his desire to find the perfect physical body temple to sexpress himself within, he also is hoping for more than sensual gratification.

Most humans hope to find their soul's mate. They want to find their soul's place. In their yearning to find this wonderful affinity, passion brings some individuals together who should never have touched a body with whom they have no rhythm or harmonic balance. Sister's POV is not wearing a welcome sign inviting any and every hopeful to worship inside her temple walls.

The Precious Omnipotent Vagina must be venerated, a place for worship. Wombman has her life's origin, her mysteries and secrets within this holy way. It is an altar on which the seeds of life are placed. When she is conceived and evolves to bring forth the source of all life, eternity becomes present within her body. Wombman's body promises joys, a way for man to come home, and a hope for soul's contentment. In other words, this precious place is a rare area, an entrance through which life enters and a living soul is birthed.

Precious Omnipotent Vagina is truly the most sacred place within the universe. Wombman is a universe unto herself yet life cannot become a living presence unless Wombman and her man are united.

Remember, POV belongs to you, Beloved. Most High power created this place of eternal life's entrance within you. Gave it to you special. This makes Wombman wonderfilling, doesn't it? After all, human life emerged from within your First World Mother's living womb and all who are breathing pays homage to her existence. What about you? Are you honoring your Mother when you attempt to bring unworthy souls into heaven's gates? Some Sisters have tried to set world records without really understanding the divine privilege bestowed within them. No Sister has to open the gates of heaven to those who are undeserving. She holds the powerful key to the mysteries of eternity. Directly within you is a queendom which has lasting power.

It is a choice matter when Sister is selective. Wombman has been dispossessed and POV deserves rest for all the weariness Sister has endured. Precious Omnipotent Vagina is a place of true endearment. Every BabySisterGirlDaughter must be taught the worthiness of her life, which can be shortened if Wombman dares to forget her calling. Sisters must exalt their sacred wombs and acknowledge their Personal Points Of View when speaking about their lives and the mysteries which come from within these beautiful bodies of First World Creation.

Your words must be spoken with respectful intent, not fear, when Precious Omnipotent Vagina is extolled. Daughters must be taught to revere the divinely powerful instrument God has bestowed between their thighs. Beloved, Precious Omnipotent Vagina is a place of worship.

God has created and bestowed this magnificent pathway to new worlds and divine life to you; therefore, this spiritual *way* is not to be taken for granted. Wombman's sacred place is hated by some and desired by many. Wars have been started because of its existence, duels fought to prove and protect man's honor because of his hopeful claim to your sacred symbol. Men have killed to gain control of this small but majestic territory, yet they could never own it. Monies are paid, and some pay dearly, nearly with their blood simply to have a taste of its power.

POV has also been used and misused as a powerful negotiation tool, an instrument to bring governments down and to make or break a human's will. First World Daughter, your Precious Omnipotent Vagina is never to be placed on a betting table nor is it to be used to ensnare. How many meetings have been delayed because of the POV? It is not a web for deceit nor is it to be shared with defeatists. How many huge deals have been lost because the deal maker has been entrapped within POV? Wombman can become a temptress simply by extending the promise of entry into her living space. Have you misapplied your power source and negated its resourcefulness? Have you given access to your POV believing it is the way to riches and success? Are you wealthy, Sister? What is your gain? Have you sold your POV for little or nothing, gaining zero for all its worth? POV is not a free agent nor is it a place where liberties should be excercized. POV is a delicacy, a delectable treat.

Your living room, a womb with a view, is at the very end of what many hope could become theirs. Every body would love to find rest in the queen's home. Would you put a sign upon your breast advertising your POV as a room for rent? Would you allow dirt, filth and grime to seek refuge within your queendom? At all times Precious Omnipotent Vagina is yours, Beloved. Even in marriage the POV belongs to you. Sister, and Sister alone, has the controlling power to designate who should enter.

Breathe, Beloved, breathe. Take a moment and listen to Divine Spirit and recognize the power God has given to you as a female human. Your body has been desired since life's inception. *It is still desirable.* Just because you are the object of attention does not mean Precious Omnipotent Vagina will be treated delicately or with affection. Sister must not be so quick to open her life to inconsideration: Maniacs are running rampant. How many of you can recall having POV bumped in the night and come dawn your whole body is aching? What have you done to yourself, Sister? You race to get what you believe is the best meal and as soon as you taste it, bitterness overpowers you. What have you done in the name of lust while seeking love? Precious Omnipotent Vagina is at risk. Her life is threatened and love is in question.

Moments of vaginal lust does not love provide. Precious Omnipotent Vagina requires sweetness, considerate and careful attention and must be given all the reverence due a living room. *It is a room for life. It is a sacred space which must be loved.* When was the last time you directed specific attention to this holy place? Do you speak about its hallowed walls to those younger SisterGirlsDaughters, allowing them opportunity to know how divine this delicate place of First World Wombman is? Does your loving man know anything about this place other than his will to come in and get out? Does your presence allow him time to understand how important your life is? You are more than a vagina with eyes. **Sister, do you love your vagina?**

Help Yourself, Sister. Check yourself. Think about your POV. Remind yourself of her holiness and get a firm grasp. Know where the internal path is leading you. Wake up, Beloved. Don't go to sleep now that we are speaking to you about life investing. Your Precious Omnipotent Vagina is a place of veneration. It is Spirit's sacred point of viewing.

Cleanliness is next to godliness. Sister has heard these words of wisdom. Sister is also warned: This special place is not to be shared with grimy, grungy, or stinky partners. Your POV is as precious as platinum and diamonds. Within your sacred space is a genuine pearl.

Love the Lord with the majesty of your soul, Sister. Spirit declares your life as majestic. None can enter her soul's portals if they are unclean, unworthy and without dignity, otherwise, Daughter, keep your doors shut tightly. Behold, we have placed before you an open door no man can close and many may attempt to enter. The invitation must come from you, Beloved. Your life environment is a jewel God has created so that all the worlds may see Divine Spirit's limitless power working. Know where Precious Omnipotent Vagina is, God lives.

Eternal life will make itself known. Some Sisters will birth and some will not. Those who birth lovingly, despite pain and remarkable agility of POV, are bringing forth a *holy order*. First World ascendants, BabyChildren of Blackness must be nurtured, cared for, and held in great esteem.

Beloved, Divine Spirit gives this new world charge/holy order to you and the BrotherFathers. You must respect penis and Precious Omnipotent Vagina. Know your worthiness. Fail to flaunt your vital bodies. Compromise not your souls; live with reverence and honor for those who were born and have died for your divine right to birth sacred souls into the new world.

Wake up, children. Wake up. Wombman, extend reverence to your loving BrotherManHusbandPartnerNuruturingBest Friend. When it is time to come together in spiritual worship, the gates of heaven will be opened to pour out blessings. Precious Omnipotent Vagina will be a source for rejoicing. POV is your claim to posterity.

BECOMING "MAKING LOVE"

Here is your invitation to enjoy your intimate worship time. With sexpressing you are acknowledging a powerful sensual sensation created for life and love and it dwells within your body temple.

Help Yourself by becoming *making love*. Everything you do can be good. You can become enraptured by assisting your loving partner to know what is fulfilling to you. When you are together imagine your loving partner is a mirror and what you are seeing is your reflection. Beloved, you are free to see your loving moves as those which help to make your most intimate moments stimulating and pleasurable, enjoyable and sexually healing. You are lovingly releasing without stress.

Receiving the best out of personal intimacy means you are willing to become one with yourself as you are reveling in your living sextasy.

109
▼▼▼

Intimate Worship and ritual time is when you relax with your loving partner in a perfumed bath or shower. Create your loving atmosphere by using fragrant oils and herbs, delicious scents and personal things which entice and enrapture. You and your partner can create a living room overflowing with love. You can also create a sensual environment by sweet talking, orally communicating what satisfies you. And perhaps you will select certain foods enjoyable to your taste and beautiful flowers complemented by candlelight and music, erotic writings or whatever stimulates you.

Beloved, every loving feeling, all things pleasant and imaginable begins within you. So when you are feeling sexually creative and before you begin making ready for those moments of intimacy, **Help Yourself** by remembering your first responsibility is sexual protection. Respect yourself, your loving partner and your lives.

Committing to **relaxing and loving myself** is my eighth step. **Self Improvement** is your key! Your command word: **Happiness**.

10

Souls Crying Out

Spirit helps us when we are available to help ourselves.
We are our NationCommunityFamily.
We are Ascendants of those souls crying out.

As I sit here I can hear Holy Spirit saying, "Souls of your people are crying for restitution. Help them to find their peace, Daughter!"

I was in meditation and words came through clearly, repeating **Souls Crying Out!** Voices were sounding in my blood. My veins were hot and I could hear them calling my name: June. June. June. June. Repeatedly they were crying, calling my name. I felt the pain of my people, those living in eternity and those who are living today.

114

I know we were forced to be ashamed of whom we believed we were, conscripted to dwell in mental and physical degradation because of European decisions to enslave us. This tragic decision has us bearing an overwhelming psychological burden; a revolving thought of not ever being good enough regardless of what our human achievements are. We are carrying the burden of the *lowest esteem worldwide*, a spiritual heaviness no other humans have had to endure.

Why is this blighted despair within the mental body of the Black ascendant? We **disobeyed** God.

As we come into awareness of who we are and who we were, and now that we are determined to do everything, with our God power, to secure a better world for those who are coming, it is imperative that we not allow any humans to desecrate us.

Never again should be our rallying cry! We must repudiate being downgraded simply because any human or any specific group, including ourselves, dares to create negative studies and statistics about us. We are doing enough self destroying. Why should we give security to any humans bent on keeping us in low states of mental, spiritual and physical bondage? Why should we justify decayed thinking, wallowing in decadence simply to comply with futuristic numbers supposedly confirming our disrespect of life?

Souls are crying out for us to stop murdering ourselves and others. Are we so debased that we would do everything in our human power to kill our souls? It is imperative that we recall our vigilant ancestors. It is imperative that we Black folk remain in a state of vigilance regarding our future. We have work to complete and we cannot do a thing until we learn to respect one another. *Where self respect is nonexistent, life cannot continue.* Wake up, children!

We hunger for historical and cultural knowledge: We can find this knowledge by research and study. When we are dedicated to our development through education and find all words of truth beneficial to our self–esteem and our understanding of our shortcomings, we are accused of being radical. When we uncover information which contributes to truth and understanding of our history, our power and growth as a people, we are defiled and accused of being militant or rewriting *his* story.

Our brains are aflame, burning for want of knowledge and information regarding our current conditions. Our human spirits are clamoring for inspirational support and we, in our determination to remain ignorant, are seemingly open for destitution. We are spiritually impoverished and it seems we are doing all we can to do injury to our current circumstances. Are we so willing to be allies and copartners with those whom we know to be our destroyers? Look in your own backyard to see who is heaving filth and rottenness onto your steps. Do they favor you? Are they holding you in great esteem? Is love evident?

GO AWAY

Why are we so willing to sell ourselves to the lowest bidder? Why are we so adamant about selling our Brothers and Sisters' souls to any denigrating substances? We are not training to be conquerors. We aren't defeating any enemies; we are providing them with souls. It is ridiculous screaming about what others are not doing when we are doing worse to ourselves. Some African inheritors are quite conceited in their ignorance. We are our own worst enemies!

Are we believing we have no intelligence, self worth or value unless our heads are grafted onto shoulders of pale complexioned persons? Do we suddenly become intellectual when integrated or formerly off limit venues are made available to us? What is wrong with our thinking? What are we processing through our brains into our emotional bodies? Are we still feeling emotional trauma from leftover enslavement? Do we **choose** to be **free?** Or are we **beggars?** Are we awaiting sanctioning from those who believe they are heirs to Manifest Destiny or are we capable of creating our own? How many of us require outside assistance to destroy our lives? Will we continue maiming, raping and murdering our minds and bodies simply because this is all we believe we can do?

What is ailing the Black man and Wombman? How do we diagnose our illnesses? Are you or anyone you know grieving? Do you know the reason for your sadness? How do we find remedy for our disgust of and distrust among ourselves? How can we heal our lives, our children and our ancestral pain? Don't you want to do more about this? Are you afraid to do something to effectively establish our righteous dominion within this earth? Is more and more rhetoric, meetings and convening our answer? What do you believe you must do to effectively stimulate positive change today, or are you still holding on to hopelessly aggravating nonsolutions?

The resolving ain't no political issue. Healing our plight might be dangerous to those within our own racial group who believe they are secure. They do not want to disturb their social standing. They don't want to raise issues which could draw attention to their **minority** problems.

We have many among our own who are humming, "Do just pass us by." We don't want to hear nothing or see nobody who would cause us to think about our blackness. And souls crying out? We don't want to hear the sounds of our own voices, let alone anything which will make us mindful of being from the Blackness. We do not choose to be reminded of who we used to be because of who we believe we are.

We have individuals passing so they can achieve freedom. They don't want to be nigras and they sure cannot be Europeans, but they are hopeful. They are more immersed in doing something about their seemingly tragic destiny than we who are communally mired in daily frustrations about our living situations.

This is why our youth are choosing to die. This is why countless humans are selecting inhumane activities. Death and destruction are not our allies. Death and destruction shall not be our legacy. Those who choose not to become involved with our spiritual uniting are allowed to kill themselves. Just leave the rest of us to our powerful charge: **Life**.

For those who are afraid of succeeding and progressing for business and ownership, go away. Do not cause nor create hindrance and barriers for the rest of us. We deserve our good. We deserve to create and have the best and we are willingly open to establishing this for ourselves and for those whom we honor. Any who choose to fall by the wayside and are refusing to be contributors in establishing our greatness, go away. We do not request nor require your negative input nor your killing ideas. Go away. Close your ears, eyes, minds and hearts to self–fulfilling progress. Deny presence of God and Holy Spirit. Go way far from us. Leave families and loving ones because you don't believe in anything anyway. Git on out and way far from life. Run so you won't hear souls crying out. Run so you won't hear your own voice praying. Get away from everything if you can.

SAVING OURSELVES

Souls are crying out. This very second your soul is a witness to horrifying and terrible images. Your soul is calling your name, begging to be liberated and no longer inundated with festering violence. We are and must be held accountable for our evil ways and our determination to hold onto fear and insecurities. *Black folk are not human cesspools.* We are not harbingers of bad news. We must not fester like running sores. The God we know has not condemned us to hell. We can move out of this mess immediately.

Souls are crying out telling us to accept our ability to

change our circumstances by acknowledging our spiritual, political and economic power. We are yelping, scrambling and looking for a great European savior to raise us from our grave situations. We have no one to blame when we step into sinkholes. Black people must be willing to accept the onus of our personal debts and the things we have allowed to come upon us. We can move out of these messes immediately by changing the ill ways in which we view ourselves and our conditions in life. It is our responsibility to get our own house—Nation CommunityFamilySelf—in order. If you choose to believe you must abide in hell then so be it; however, if you want heaven while on earth then it is our duty to honor the Divine Spirit within each of us.

Who are we looking to for our Nation's salvation? An uninterested society who mentally slams doors when we try to enter? What makes us hope anyone is responsible for saving us now? No one is responsible for uplifting us but we. **No one can save us but ourselves.**

Wake up, Black souls. Wake and hear the sounds of our ancestral voices crying out for us to stop our self destruction and rise to life. You can hear them calling your name. Listen.

The blood rumbling through your veins tell you our ancestors died that you might respect and honor our aliveness. And what are you doing? Wallowing in fear, racing to shoot, snort, smoke, stab, punch, kick, and become drunk in vile behavior? Is this our reality?

It seems we don't want to be anything but **no things**. Is this the only life we claim? Are we yet harboring shame because of our previous enslavement? Are we going to insist on and keep helping others to build enslavement camps to house the Black criminal minded (future projections) and our insantified? Yes, insantified. They are not sanctified; they are bordering on insanity and they are not conscious of their own ability to transform their unholy conditions.

While we breathe we still have those who are looking for a pat on the head, selling our secrets for a watermelon seed and having not a plot of land in which to plant it. Why are we so anxious for everyone to know what we are getting ready to do? We don't know or, perhaps, we don't want to do anything beneficial in silence. We want to do this, tell the world about that, tell them our awareness has come and that we are no longer dumb and no longer cherish stupidity and lackadaisical attitudes. We don't believe we can achieve without having to yell our progressive resolutions to the world.

SPIRIT NEVER DIES

It is time to harness our dollars, putting them on hold by securing and establishing our banking power. We know it is time to invest and enfold our communities into our hearts by supporting and helping those who need to be educated in every manner possible. *Egos must be thrown out.* We must surrender our human will to God, Maker and Creator of our aliveness.

Divine Spirit is our security and our good spiritual consciousness creates prosperity. Our brains are not dulled to progress. **We have to believe in ourselves**. We have to reform our thinking and form a new Nation with God and Holy Spirit. We must service our own.

Folk are getting angered now because the nigra is awakening. Are these the remnants of those Black bucks and high hipped mammies? Who has taught these slave minded individuals to think? Who has given them incentive to believe and hope they can trust one another? Who has dared to give them incentive to unite and make use of their professional talents? And who inspires them to understand the meaning of economic power? Who and what power has made them aware of their spiritual qualities? *Whoever it is must be destroyed*. Murdered AssassinatedHungBurnedLynchedAbortedDopedoutDragged Drunktified. Whatever must be done just get rid of the powerfully positive Influencer.

Humph, that mover and shaker is **Divine Spirit**. The powerfilling presence of God will not be stilled. Spirit cannot be killed. It is life eternal. **Spirit Never Dies**.

This eternality is responding to our silent prayers and hears our souls crying out. Restitution begins with us. It begins with our thinking worthiness and with respect of our own talents, our lives, and our children.

Reparations begins with honoring our fallen foot soldiers, warrior souls who trod broken ground and our brave spiritual leaders, teachers, authors, and orators who impressed their lives on the world. It is requested that we venerate our past, without it we would not be alive to make positive change manifest today.

Souls be crying out for our blood. Not tainted or infested with vileness but our bleeding for victory, bleeding for our awakening, our humane sensibility and our strengthening courage. We have got to have heart. We cannot shut ourselves down and we cannot blow ourselves off like steam.

We have to stop supporting our children who are murdering each other. We must condemn their romanticized dreams about fine funerals, elaborate burials and ornate crypts. We must blot out their fantasies about stretch limousines, fabulous wreaths, and floral blankets, folk falling out (mainly for fear of not being able to pay for all the fantastical murderous dreams) youthful companions and girlfriends screaming for deceased to come back. Ministers, priest, Imams and family members speaking about how he or she was felled so early in the prime of life. Whose life? Some of these destined to be young good–looking corpses better get jobs and purchase burial insurance because the majority of bereaved families are tremendously burdened by debts, concerned about rent and having food to eat. What is your living about Black people?

Souls be crying out for us to refrain from our wicked ways. Black purveyors of souls need to know about ownership. How many illegal weapons are you buying and selling? Where is your international connections to illegal drug supplies? What color are the hands counting the enormous profits being made from the plague of Black deaths? How many boats, ships and planes do you own? How many cruise yachts, Lear jets, government sponsored transport planes? How many South American acres/plantations are you controlling? How many land grants has the drug masters deeded to you? Are you free to dine with his family, be entertained in his home, stroll the avenues of high–priced shops and restaurants? How many huge homes, small guest houses, private rooms in hotels and beaches are you laying back on? Are you stagnating in European colonial consciousness, proud to be a vampire draining blood from the souls of your people?

How many of us have built schools, purchased hospitals or own news organizations? How many convention centers, arenas and halls do we own? How many have invested in or purchased television stations showing our beleaguered and contorted Black faces thrown against a police car window? How many cops know you personally? How many of you can read the disturbing statistics written about your lack of knowledge, your lack of morals and your intentional lack of progress? Are you a slave or are you mastering knowledge and common sense?

Souls crying out, weeping enough tears to create seas, rivers, and oceans. Why do our people shed so many tears?

Why are we wringing our hands in sorrow? Why are we not more joy filled?

Why are we so committed to self hatred? Don't we have enough hostility brought to us simply because of lies about our enslavement and the colors of our skin? Why are we intent on destroying our families, communities and our Nation?

The world's sight is blinded against and insensitive to our plight. Most who are dwelling within European consciousness, including many of First World ancestry, do not believe Blacks have suffered spiritual, mental and physical breakdown. We don't speak these words facetiously, nor do we take lightly what is being expressed. Many people of African heritage are being aroused and are beginning to check ourselves affirmatively, while others are grasping for any reasons to keep us in our self–imposed dysfunction.

How dare Black folk seek to make amends to remedy their ailing NationCommunityFamily? How dare Black folk seek to heal themselves? The nigras are getting smart now, so lets claim reverse paranoia.

We cannot prevent any humans from having their fears but we cannot allow their fears to cancel our faith and believing. We must trust our power to create and define our determinative plans, going forth and implementing them triumphantly.

A CALL FOR TRIUMPHANT BLACK FOLK

Today ·God is calling for Black folk who are fearless, strengthened and astute. You can hear your name being sounded out; therefore, it is imperative that you believe you are qualified to answer the calling. Do not deny hearing souls crying out because you are truly needed for our coming forth.

We cannot afford to be idle and complaining. We are responsible for being dedicated to our future and our new world order. We cannot afford complacency and wild attitudes. Ignorance is detrimental; intellect and intelligence are necessary for our successes. We need greatness oriented humans, spiritually minded individuals. We need First World ascendants, Black men and Wombman willing to reach within and utilize every faculty God has provided us with to be accomplished builders of God's spiritual foundation.

> *Spirit helps us when we are available to help ourselves.*
> *We are our NationCommunitiesFamilies.*
> *We are Ascendants of those souls crying out.*

Let us respond with respect. Let us step forward with honor. Let us be the creators of our future. We are starting today.

As I breathe, I am hearing Spirit saying, "Souls of your people are crying out for restitution. Help them to claim relief, Daughter!" I thank God I am willing to be the definition of the answer. *This is a call for triumphant Black folk!!!!!*

11

I Am Thankful

Are you breeding hostilities or are you breathing grace?
Do you vex a body or are you a cleansing Wombman?
Are you a contentious Sister or do you bring peace?

I am thankful for our SisterDaughters and to our Brother Sisters. I am thankful for our ought to be Sisters and our misunderstood. I am thankful to Sisters who stood on mountain tops, rocks and sea waves. I am thankful for Sisters who hold themselves and others steady in howling winds. I am grateful to our unflappable Sisters who refused to be bothered during times of turmoil. Our *I shall not, I shall not be moved* Sisters.

I am thankful to our bleeding Sisters who endured whips and chains, breathing in pain and holding their own baby Sisters and the owner's babies. I am thankful for *knowing* Sisters guiding us in spirit. They are God's gifts, bringing courage, confidence and never confusion.

Oh, Lord, there is deepness here. My soul sighs with thankfulness for those living eternally. Our forbearers still looking out for us, surrounding and helping in times of needful reflection. I am thankful their torches are ablaze, guiding us into ways of decency, kindness and respect.

I am thankful because I am of them. They knew we'd be born. Are we appreciating Sisters?

Count yourself among those who are blessed and who are blessing others. Know because you are born you are blessed. Now is the time to count your blessings, *number your accomplishments one by one, those you have and those to come.*

As First World Creation, Black Wombman, we are birthed to recognize new Sisters coming. And we have to know our **Isness**: **I**nseparable in **S**pirit. **N**urturing **E**nsuring our **S**piritual **S**ecurity. To the willing and want to be Sisters, I am thankful for you today. In appreciation and honor of our ancestors, the Spirit has given these Commandments to all their First World ascendants:

> *Do not indulge hate filled humans.*
> *Do not go into unrighteous environments.*
> *Do not invite anger into your heart.*
> *Do not threaten your breasts by suckling snakes.*
> *Do not greet evil's sons nor daughters with glee.*
> *Do not give safe harbor to intrusive individuals.*
> *Do not speak peace with a liar.*
> *Do not entertain a blamer.*
> *Do not send sexual energies to undesirables.*
> *Do not tweak a licentious person's curiosity.*
> *Do not confuse enslavement for endearment.*
> *Do not make laziness an art.*
> *Do not languish in filth nor consort with filth minded humans.*
> *Do not abide where your breathing is threatened.*
> *Do not support mind controlling lovers.*
> *Do not surrender your tenderness to an abuser.*

Do not seek comfort in vicious circles.

Do not share laughter with child beaters.

Do not open your doors to gamblers.

Do not subject yourself to harassment.

Do not reveal your valuables to braggarts.

Do not spend money on a shiftless person.

Do not invest your breath in untrustworthy humans.

Do not stand for disrespect.

Do not dine with a rude host.

Do not share your sweets with cheaters.

Do not honor a thief.

Do not give service to a debtor.

Do not live in fear.

Do not pay homage to a lawless human.

Do not sacrifice your loving life to carelessness.

Do not cherish stinginess.

Do not look for compassion from a batterer.

Do not confuse gossip for wisdom.

First World Creation, Black Wombman, know your **Isness**.
I am thankful!

Signature: _____

Committing to **never forgetting who I am** is my empowering step. Knowing **I am original substance** of God's Divine and loving Spirit is your key. Your command words: **Veneration**. **Commandment**. **Nation**.